HUSTLING GOD

D0390607

Also by M. Craig Barnes

Sacred Thirst

WHY WE WORK
SO HARD FOR WHAT
GOD WANTS TO GIVE

HUSTLING
GOD

M. Craig Barnes

ZondervanPublishingHouse
Grand Rapids, Michigan

A Division of HarperCollinsPublishers

Hustling God
Copyright © 1999 by M. Craig Barnes

Requests for information should be addressed to:

🔖 ZondervanPublishingHouse
Grand Rapids, Michigan 49530

Library of Congress Cataloging-in-Publication Data

Barnes, M. Craig.
    Hustling God : why we work so hard for what God wants to give /
M. Craig Barnes.
       p.   cm.
    Includes bibliographical references.
    ISBN 0-310-23952-4 (Softcover)
    1. Christian life—Presbyterian authors. 2. Jacob (Biblical patriarch)
I. Title.
BV4501.2.B382856   1999
248.4'851—dc21   98-51433
                                                    CIP

All Scripture quotations, unless otherwise indicated, are taken from the *New Revised Standard Version of the Bible,* copyright © 1989 by the Division of Christian Education of the National Council of Churches of Christ in the United States of America and are used by permission. All rights reserved.

All rights reserved. No part of this publication may be reproduced, stored in a retrieval system, or transmitted in any form or by any means—electronic, mechanical, photocopy, recording, or any other—except for brief quotations in printed reviews, without the prior permission of the publisher.

Published in association with Alive Communications, Inc., 7680 Goddard Street, Suite 200, Colorado Springs, CO 80920

Interior design by Sherri L. Hoffman

Printed in the United States of America

00 01 02 03 04 05 /❖ DC/ 10 9 8 7 6 5 4 3 2 1

For the people of The National Presbyterian Church,

whom I dearly love

CONTENTS

ONE

BORN TO STRIVE

When her time to give birth was at hand, there were twins in her womb. The first came out red, all his body like a hairy mantle; so they named him Esau. Afterward his brother came out, with his hand gripping Esau's heel; so he was named Jacob.

GENESIS 25:24–26

Everybody has a dream. Perhaps you don't even know exactly what the dream is, but still it runs your life. Your dream is what gets you up in the morning. It is what you pursue every day of your life. The dream is what drove you to leave your parents' home, get an education, and find a job. It's the reason you moved from one city to another. It led you into relationships, and it led you out of them. Every important decision you have made in life has been determined by how close it gets you to the dream. The problem is that the dream keeps moving. It's a hard thing to catch.

Sometimes we find that other people are living our dreams. Everywhere *they* turn, *our* dreams come true for them! That's how Jacob viewed Esau. Esau stumbled into every blessing the world had to offer and took it all for granted.

For the rest of us, life is a chore. We have to strive to realize our dreams. That is why we can easily relate to Jacob. His story describes how life really is for those of us who are determined to make something of our lives. Believing that nothing is naturally coming our way, we determine to go out and make our dreams come true.

I now know that is the best way in the world to mess up your life.

The only good dreams come from God. And God insists on simply giving them to us. The most important dreams are blessings such as being loved, having a child, discovering your purpose in life, or finding a friend who will stick with you through anything, even the truth. Yet, if we insist on hunting down these sacred gifts, we prevent ourselves from enjoying them. In fact, that is what happens every time we try to earn what we can only receive as a blessing.

That was the great flaw in Jacob's life. It is in mine too. And maybe even in yours.

YOUR PREFERRED TWIN

Jacob and Esau were far from being identical twins. They did not look like each other at all, but they were linked by a great struggle. Their father, Isaac, wasn't all that significant a figure except that he was their link to the blessings of life that Jacob so desperately wanted. The problem was that everyone assumed these blessings would naturally fall to Esau, the firstborn. Everyone, that is, except the twins' mother, Rebekah, who was determined to help her baby get any advantage he could in life.

As the story goes, when she was carrying the twins in her womb, they created such a ruckus that she thought she was going to die. When she prayed about this, God informed her that it would make sense that she was having a hard time because "Two nations are in your womb, and two peoples born of you shall be divided; the one shall be stronger than the other, the elder shall serve the younger."[1] We have no record of Rebekah's telling Isaac about this promise from God. It seems they kept a lot of secrets from each other. Later in the story it becomes obvious that this family is as dysfunctional as they come, and that only intensifies the struggle of the twins.

Like Jacob, we all have a twin. Esau isn't just Jacob's older brother. He is the person who is like us, but better. From our earliest recollection we are measuring ourselves against some Esau, some image of what we think we should be. We knock ourselves out to fill the image, to become more like the twin who haunts us through life. It's the only way we know how to get his blessing, the one we believe should have been ours in the first place.

But no matter what we do, it is never good enough because we believe Esau would have done it better. When our parents tried sincerely to affirm us as children, what we actually heard was, "That's not bad ... for Jacob." Even if we had no siblings, or even if we were the star child of the family, we still had to compete with Esau who was the better image of ourselves. When we achieved success later in life, regardless of how good it was, we continued to taint every celebration by whispering to ourselves, "Yeah, but Esau would have done it better."

We are very ambivalent about this twin, finding that our hearts are filled with both hate and envy. We hate the fact that Esau is what we are not, but we want so much to be like him that he takes on the power of a god in our lives. For that reason Esau has become an evil twin. In our minds we have turned him into a taskmaster whom we will never satisfy.

JACOB: AN AMERICAN STORY

Jacob's name means "striver" or "hustler." He had so much drive and ambition that he could have been the poster child for the American Dream. Our society has always admired those of the huddled masses who came to this country with little, but through hard work were able to make something of themselves.

I know about that drive. I was raised on Long Island, which is divided by a long railroad track. Those on the north shore enjoy affluent communities where Mom drives the Lexus to the train station to drop off her husband who commutes into New York City. She then deposits the kids at private schools and races off to her tennis lessons. When time permits she joins her friends in a little charity work where they raise money for those less fortunate than themselves. It is a life of privilege, comfort, and enviable blessings. At least, that was the view we had from the other side of the railroad tracks where I was raised.

Our dads, if we had them, worked hard at blue-collar jobs, if they had them. We weren't unhappy and certainly didn't consider ourselves poor, but we knew our opportunities were limited. Some of my friends were content to live out their lives in that community where the most they could hope for was a job, a nice tract home, and a son who would someday be the star of the high school football team. But others of us were determined to do whatever it took to escape the place where we started in life. Like Jacob, I knew that there were those who had it made and those who would have to make it happen. I was in the second group.

I now have a great family, a beautiful home, and a good job. I am the pastor of The National Presbyterian Church in Washington, D.C. It certainly isn't the largest church in our denomination, but it does have a rather large steeple, which is really important to us strivers. I worked hard to get through college, seminary, and graduate school. I've knocked myself out to do well as an associate pastor, and then as the pastor of a middle-sized church, to finally become the senior pastor of a large church.

By every measurable standard of life, I have crossed the railroad tracks. But none of the happiness I have found in life has come from the things I achieved. All of it came from the gifts I received along the way.

Not long into my tenure as the pastor of our church, I realized I was equipped with just the right neurosis to lead our congregation. We are a church that is jam-packed with Jacobs. There is really very little blue blood in our ranks. Washington is a city whose favorite myth is that anyone can come from anywhere to make something of himself or herself here. From the politicians on down to the lowly interns who slave away at copy machines all day, we are a city filled with strivers. In that regard, we are an All-American town.

There is a great deal of cynicism about Washington, but we are a city created by the rest of the nation. There is nothing really unique about life inside the Beltway. What I have seen in my own life, and in the lives of those who fill the pews of my congregation, is pretty typical of what can be found in most communities around our country. The ambition to grab enough power to re-create our lives is a national phenomenon.

We are a nation of wanna-bes. We want to be successful and respected. We want to be loved and cared for and maybe even happy. We know that we only get one shot at life, and we are determined to get it right because we'll be dead for a long time. We may put our faith in different things, but most of us are try-ing really hard to get to that elusive place where life will finally be good enough.

PLANS THAT DON'T WORK

Some of us are logging in massive hours at work each week, hoping that the boss will stop by our desk and say, "You're really doing a good job here." To get that affirmation we cope with meetings that drag on forever and accomplish little, appointments with people who have to see us "right away," computers that crash when we need them the most, phones that never stop ringing, faxes requiring immediate attention, and a legion of little pink pieces of paper that demand, "Please Call!" At the end of these long days we struggle to find time for our spouses and children, aging parents, friends, and houses that always need attention. As we fulfill all these duties we wonder if we should cancel the coun-seling appointment we made to talk about our harried lives.

And the pace is no different on the home front. Stay-at-home parents have the most demanding schedules of all. They ferry kids to school, soccer practice, piano lessons, and visits to the ortho-dontist. In between, they shop for groceries, take the dog to the vet, catch an occasional workout, maintain friendships, and do volunteer work. On top of that, they somehow clean the house, prepare the meals, and keep up with the laundry, which multiplies as the only miracle they ever see.

Being a Christian doesn't seem to change any of this. Actually, it just adds another layer of expectations on us. Not only do we want to maintain our many commitments, but we also want the approval of the heavenly Father who may one day say, "Well done, good and faithful servant." So in addition to all the other things that it takes to live well, Christians also attend worship on Sunday and get to committee meetings, Bible studies, choir practice, and youth group. Some will even find time to volunteer in the soup kitchens or homeless shelters.

Sadly, the statistics claim that Christians are failing at life just like their secular neighbors. The divorce rate, the percentage of kids who get in trouble, and the numbers who complain of their unhappiness is exactly the same as those who don't bother with all that religious activity.

We think that Christians ought to have the best families, the most successful careers, and, of course, the best plan for being happy. Our plan, however, is precisely what is not working. Christians hate to admit this, but lots of non-Christians have lives that sure look as happy as ours do. If getting ahead in this life is the reason for all of our striving, then as the apostle Paul said, "we are of all people most to be pitied."[2]

I believe there is actually a deeper, more spiritual motivation to our striving. What we are after is not beating out Esau. He does drive us a little crazy, but actually he is beside the point. The thing we really want has more to do with God. We've inherited the promise to Jacob, which is still ringing in our ears, "You will be blessed." We'll do anything to get that blessing. In fact, we are trying to do everything at the same time, thinking that if we just don't drop one of the spinning plates, well, then we will earn the blessing. What we keep forgetting is that God promised to *give* it to us, and one day we wake up to the awful realization that we ran right by the blessing.

A woman sits beside a bed, stroking the hair of her dying mother who has fallen into a deep coma. Things have not been good between them for a long time. She meant to work on that. But there was her demanding career, her own children to raise, and so many pressing appointments. There was always a pressing appointment. Now she would give the world if only the dying mother could hear her say, "I love you, Mom." But it is too late.

A young man cradles his newborn daughter. He remembers how hard his own life was and swears that this kid will never be in need. So he throws himself into his work. As the years pass by he loses count of how many piano recitals and swim meets he missed. After a while he stops apologizing for all the weekends that were lost to the office. Then one day he finds himself driving the daughter to college. He can't believe it. He wonders where the time went. He wonders how the child grew up so fast. He wonders how he forgot to give her the most important thing—himself. But now she is gone.

A woman buries her husband. As the casket is lowered into the grave she remembers the plan they had to work hard through the middle years and enjoy life in the later years. But he died right after retirement, and now she is left alone. She curses herself for being so stupid.

These are not uncaring people. They are good people who are driven to get the life of their dreams. But they tried too hard, and one day realized that they have passed by the things that mean the most to them. It is easier to recognize a blessing after it is gone.

It doesn't have to end that way. It is possible to enjoy every day of life as an unfolding mystery filled with more gifts than we can hold. But most of us are too afraid of mystery and too busy to find it in ordinary places. We are so obsessed with what we do not have, we can't see the value of what we have been given. The blessings from God are usually hidden in very plain packages. They come wrapped in things like an evening meal at the kitchen table with someone you love, a child you see playing in the backyard while you're doing the dishes, a great conversation with a friend at the Laundromat. In these earthen vessels are found the treasure of God's love.

THE BLESSING

To be blessed is to discover that God cherishes us more deeply than we do ourselves. This love is so strange and overwhelming that it transforms our lives. It leaves us not as different people, but as our true selves without any of the pretense we picked up with our envy of Esau. Thus, to receive God's blessing is to come home to a place we have never been, but where, from the moment we arrive, we know we belong. It is the place where we are unconditionally loved.

One of the Hebrew words for blessing is *ashar*. It means "to be made happy on the right path."[3] When Jesus used the word "blessed" in the Beatitudes he claimed that the right path was the opposite one from the one we would expect. "Blessed are the poor in spirit, for theirs is the kingdom of heaven. . . . Blessed are the meek, for they will inherit the earth."[4] He could also have said, "Blessed are the receivers, for they know they are cherished." The right path isn't the road that we climb up, it is the road that God climbs down to bless us.

Abraham was one of the first persons in the Bible to discover that a blessing is found only on the path God gives us. That's why it is the right path and why it will ultimately make us happy. But along the way, God's path can seem pretty strange.

When we are told that God promised to "bless" Abram, as he was first named, this time the Hebrew uses the word *barak*.[5] It has the connotation of being made fruitful with lots of children. It was exactly the gift that Abram and his barren wife Sarai had always longed for. But receiving this blessing meant packing up their well-ordered life in Ur of the Chaldeans and moving to a strange new place. After arriving, they were supposed to wait on God to give them a child. So they waited ... and waited. After the years started piling up, the waiting became so unbearable that the tired old couple decided to help God produce this child.

Abram had a child with Sarai's handmaid. The birth of any child is a blessing, but the arrival of this one created enormous complications for the household. That is what usually happens when we try to help God out. Blessings are not achievements; they are gifts from heaven. So God reappeared to Abram and Sarai and told them that he really meant it. They would have a child— together. By this time they were so old it was getting funny. So funny that Abram fell on his face laughing. Another passage claims that Sarai was hiding in a tent laughing her head off at this strange God, this strange blessing, and this strange path they were on. So when the blessed child was finally born, God told them to go ahead and call him Isaac, which means laughter. Not just "ha-ha" laughter, but delighted laughter over a blessing so bizarre only God could come up with it.

After Isaac was finally born, Abraham had figured out that the real blessing was not having a son, but having a God who is faithful. Eventually he became so convinced of that, he was even willing to give Isaac up if that was what God wanted.

Those lessons in faith were lost on Jacob. For Jacob, what you see is what you get, and in spite of God's promise to give Abraham's blessing to him, our boy can't see how that is going to happen. Blessings in those days came as birthrights, and as the second son, Jacob is born without hope for the blessing. So he has his doubts. He doesn't doubt the blessing. What he doubts is that it will be a blessing for *him*.

I find that when I preach about the blessings of God, the folks in my congregation nod in general agreement. None of us really doubts that God is powerful or loving, but we are not at all sure that God really wants to bring all that power and love into our lives. I have no doubts as to whose hands are behind the formation of the skies above me. Nor do I doubt that "God so loved the world." But when I go to work, I have serious doubts that any of God's creativity or love will come my way. I sure don't say that to anyone. But why else would I arrive early and stay late, demand that the staff try harder, and keep pushing to start more programs?

In addition to the blessing, there is another voice also ringing in our ears. It is that other voice that drives us by whispering, "Sure, God can make the stars, but your life isn't going to amount to much if you don't hustle."

There is a lot we can do through hustle and resolve. We can improve our lifestyles, lose weight, achieve degrees, and make changes in our careers and relationships. But when it comes to the most important things of life, like our character, it doesn't matter how much resolve we have, we are never going to improve on that just by making a few changes. We are going to have to become a new creation.

I AM PLEASED WITH YOU

The new creation that God makes of our lives has little to do with changing us. That was our plan. God doesn't make changes. God creates. And this new creation in our lives looks an awful lot like the good creation we were intended to be from the beginning. It is only when we see the goodness of what God has formed that we will be content to receive our lives with gratitude. Until we believe it is God who created our lives, and has called all creation "good," we will continue to judge our lives as being not good enough.

Christians understand Jesus to be their blessed Savior because he reunites us to our Creator from whom we wandered away in search of self-improvement plans. As the Son of Man he brings us home to the place where we can be ourselves again. And as the Son of God he embodies the passion of a Creator dying to love us.

When Jesus began his ministry he went out into the desert wilderness where John the Baptist was leading people in a ritual of repentance. In the Bible, the desert was always seen as an in-between place. Nobody wanted to stay there because life was hard and frightening in the wilderness. Ancient people, like most of us, were city dwellers. The only reason they entered the wilderness was to get to someplace else. So it was a fitting setting for John's baptisms, where people went to leave behind the life they knew and to begin a new life as those whose sins had been washed away.

John's baptism was different from the Christian understanding. Although people would go to him to become cleansed of their sins, they knew they had a propensity to keep sinning. So the next week they would come back and be rebaptized to start again with a clean slate and to try one more time to get life right. John's religion wasn't complicated. He claimed, "It's up to you to live right. If you do, when judgment comes, you will be spared."

We like John's message. Or at least we understand it. It is a religion that keeps telling us to try harder. It is the same message we get at school and work—and maybe even at home. The reason we like it is that it appeals to something heroic in us. We would like to think that if we work hard enough, we will get life right. We want to believe that we have done a good job.

We can understand, therefore, why John was so confused the day Jesus Christ showed up in the wilderness asking to be baptized. He was supposed to be the judge who, as John warned, would blow fire down from the skies on those who weren't living right. But instead of giving fire, the Son of God gave himself when he stepped down into the waters of the Jordan River. He identified with flawed humans, who were trying to do the thing we humans do best—make a few changes. We share John's amazement. "Jesus, what are you doing here? You haven't failed. You are the standard we are trying to meet. You are the judge we are trying to satisfy. Why are you here in this place where sins are washed away?"

Jesus responded to John's objections by saying that his baptism was necessary "to fulfill all righteousness." In other words, this is the only way we will be made right. The sinless one, the judge, came to us who were lost in a sea of good intentions. In his baptism he altered our understanding of how we find hope. Now we are made right, not by trying harder, but by seeing that God is with us.

The moment Jesus emerged from under the water, the heavenly Father ripped back the skies and said, "This is my Son, the Beloved, with whom I am well pleased."[6] Nowhere in the Bible are we told that God is impressed by how hard someone is trying. No, what pleases God is that in Jesus he found you out in the wilderness, where you were trying hard to get to the right place in life. And he says, "You, too, are my son, my daughter. With you I am also well pleased." That is because in Jesus Christ we have received a new twin, not a standard of performance like Esau, but a Savior who embodies what we really are—the pleasure of God.

Do you remember how you longed as a child to hear that someone was pleased with you? No matter how hard you tried, it never seemed to be good enough. If only someone would have said, "But I love you. I am so pleased with you."

In Jesus Christ, that is exactly what your heavenly Father says.

Bruce Larson has claimed that some of us go through life listening to voices from the cellar, while others hear the voice from the balcony. From below us are the cellar influences of harsh words that were said early in our childhood: "You're not good enough. You're not pretty. You're not very smart." Although we have tried to rise above those judgments and have built very successful lives, we can still hear the voices from the past. They seep up through the floorboards and haunt us our whole life.

Others have chosen to listen to the voice from the balcony. It is the only one that can drown out the nonsense from the cellar. It is the voice of God, the heavenly Father, who is so pleased with you. He is pleased not because of what you have done but because of what Jesus has done. He found you in the wilderness and brought you home. Grace. Amazing grace born out of God's love for you.

Grace means that there isn't anything you can do to make God love you any less. What will drive you crazy is the discovery that there isn't anything you can do to make him love you any *more*, either. When it comes to the love of God, all you can do is receive it and at long last discover that your life is being made right. That is the blessing we have been yearning for since the day we were born.

In our baptism, we who follow Jesus do not baptize to wash away sins. That's hopeless and we know it, because like all of those before us, we just keep sinning. We baptize to identify ourselves with Jesus and to mark ourselves as a people who will live only by grace. Whenever the church baptizes someone, we are telling all of our stories again and again and again. It is the story of the day Jesus found us on the banks of judgment.

Every time we see a baptism we remember that we too have passed through the waters. Like the Hebrews who crossed the Red Sea, we have left slavery behind. We have passed through the wilderness. For us, baptism is now the "in-between place." It boldly proclaims we can begin anew. We are not slaves to anyone's judgment—not our parents', children's, ex-spouse's, or our boss's. We are not slaves to low self-esteem. We are not slaves to the mistakes or sins of the past. Not if we really believe in the grace that is proclaimed in the sacrament. Not if we have come to hear the voice from the balcony proclaiming, "You are my beloved, in whom I am pleased."

Your baptism is the gateway to the Promised Land. All you have to do is walk through it. Just take the first steps of faith. Walk away from judgment, and God will get so excited that he'll rip back the heavens and a little more light will shine down. There will be at least enough to show you that you are dearly blessed.

THE BLESSED FUTURE

Even before his birth, Jacob's future had already been determined by God. There was nothing conditional about the promise. God simply decided that he would bless Jacob. No matter what

he did, no matter where he roamed, no matter how hard he hustled, the blessing was waiting for him. As simple as that promise
was, Jacob could never understand it. That is because he kept
thinking that the future was determined by the decisions of the
present. The blessing claims, however, that the present is determined by the future.

We live in a society that bombards us with choices. We can
choose whom we will love, where we will live, what we believe,
and how we will spend our time. Our government lets us choose
our leaders and our politics. Our churches let us choose our worship styles. Our families let us choose what we will do for a living.
It is easy for us to think that all of these choices are critical for
determining our future. If we make good choices, then our lives
will turn out fine. And if our lives have not turned out as we
dreamed, we have only ourselves to blame. That is why Jacob hustled through every day of his life. He was certain that the only way
he could get the future he wanted was to make the choices today
that would lead him there.

The Bible claims that is exactly wrong: "For by grace you have
been saved through faith, and this is not your own doing; it is the
gift of God."[7] God has already written the end of your story. By
grace, it ends wonderfully. There isn't anything you can choose to
do that will make it end any better. If you know that the story ends
well, then the only choice that is really left is to enjoy the mystery
as it slowly unfolds. That is the path called faith.

Now, this is still asking a lot. It is asking you to choose to
understand the present, not by the options that are currently obvious but by your vision of the future. When Jacob looked only at
his present options, all he could see was that the odds were stacked
against him ever receiving anything remotely resembling a blessing. When those born on the wrong side of the tracks look at their
present opportunities, they have little reason for hope. When we
read the newspapers that describe the present condition of our
world, we have little motivation to keep working for a just society.

But when we can clearly see the future that God has already determined, then we have a very clear motivation to continue to do the right thing with our lives, believing that God will be faithful in making it a blessing.

BECOMING WHO YOU ARE

Once when I was on vacation at a deserted lake, I saw two beautiful bald eagles soaring above my head. The eagles lived in a nest on a small island near our cabin. During the week I was there, I became absolutely enraptured by these eagles. They were the most majestic and inspiring creatures I had ever seen in the wilderness. When I returned home, I started to read everything that I could find about eagles. I talked about them all the time. My poor congregation heard way too many sermons and devotionals about "mounting up with wings as eagles." I was obsessed with these great birds.

Then our local zoo announced that their eagles had eggs that were about to hatch. I couldn't wait to see the babies. Finally the big day came. I raced to the zoo to be one of the first in line to behold their beauty. But I was, well, disappointed by what I saw. They were just balls of fuzz.

If I were to take one of those fuzz balls to the rooftop and pitch it off with the command to soar, it wouldn't be a very pretty sight. But clearly, if I leave it alone, that baby bird will eventually fly. There is no question about its future, because it is an eagle. Everything that it will do from the moment it is hatched is designed to help it meet its appointed future to soar above the mountain peaks. The fact that it cannot fly today doesn't mean that it won't someday.

Eagles have to become what they are. So do Christians. There isn't much we have to do to become soaring eagles since that is what God has determined we will be. Mostly, what the spiritual disciplines teach us is how to wait on the Lord until we can spread our wings.[8]

Imagine how sad it would be if that baby eagle was adopted by a family of snakes. As its wings developed and tried to catch the wind, the snakes would say, "No, no. Don't ever spread those ugly wings. What you should do is crawl on your belly, hide under rocks, and bite anyone who scares you." Can you imagine anything more pathetic than an eagle pretending to be a snake? That's what happens when we try to get the blessing on our own.

We can never justify acting like a snake just because we live in a world that is filled with snakes. Nor can we excuse our venom by saying, "Just get used to it, because that's who I am." That is not who you are! You are God's creation, and he didn't make you angry, cynical, or deadly. You can pretend to be a snake if you insist, but God will never settle for it.

In claiming that we are the new creation of God, we are saying that in the end we will become the blessing that only he can make of us. Today, it may not be at all clear how he will do that. But that is a Savior's worry.

For now, it is enough to claim our identity as the cherished daughters and sons with whom the heavenly Father is well pleased. The more we believe that, the easier it will be to fight off the great temptation that has plagued us since our childhood—pretending to be something less than we really are.

TWO

LEARNING TO PRETEND

So he went in to his father, and said, "My father"; and
he said, "Here I am; who are you, my son?" Jacob said
to his father, "I am Esau your firstborn."

GENESIS 27:18–19

Our families have pretty strong ideas about who we should
be. Since they are led by flawed parents, some of their ideas about
our identity are also flawed. For example, we learn from an early
age that our fathers prefer Esau. We are told that Esau was a skill-
ful hunter, a man of the field. But that is not why our fathers prefer him. They prefer him because he looks like the blessing they
were expecting. For a while we may struggle against that, but in
time we learn how to pretend we are Esau. It is the only way we
know to get our father's blessing.

JACOB WAS A QUIET MAN

As the story continues we learn that Jacob was a quiet man,
living in tents.[1]

We live in a world full of noise. Our homes and cars have a
radio going constantly. Paying attention to the music is beside the
point. Its purpose is to drown out the disturbing quiet. When I
visit parishioners in the hospital, the television is rarely off. Typically it is left on while we are trying to talk, as if its function is to
prevent us from entering into a serene conversation where we will

have to deal with issues of mortality. At the office we grow accustomed to ringing phones, chatty colleagues, and lots of meetings. We even prefer it. When there are no distractions we are stuck with our thoughts, and that will scare us quicker than anything making noise in the world.

The pressure to be noisy begins at an early age, when parents try too hard to drive the quiet out of their children. After my daughter was born, I couldn't lean over her crib without lapsing into a Jerry Lewis routine, making the most absurd faces and sounds just to get a giggle out of her. When she became a teenager, I became more desperate to get her to talk with me, but had less success than when she was an infant. Her private world frightens me, not because I think she is doing something wrong in there, but just because it is private. I want her to grow up to be outstanding in the world, like Esau. How can I direct that if she doesn't let me take control of her life? Her best method of resisting that is simply to remain quiet.

As she leaves home and enters the noisy world, she will discover that if she wants to succeed in this world, she will have to give people what they want. And the people's preference for Esau is even greater than her parents'.

Like my daughter, my favorite retreat from being controlled by people is also to become quiet. When I am needed at home, I can usually be found in my office behind a shut door trying to get a little sanctuary in my tent. After a while, I get exhausted pretending that I am Esau.

Church members know when they have an introverted pastor on their hands. Most of the members of my congregation have come to terms with this limitation, but they still wish I could live more easily out in the field like Esau. So do I.

Pastors enter the ministry, not just to explore the depths of theological insight, but because we care about people. We have dedicated our lives to helping others understand their lives as a great drama with the God who loves them and is not done creating a good work with them. People get clarity about that good work from the pastor who travels with them through all the ordinary experiences of life in the world. This doesn't mean that the sermon is unimportant. It is serious business to proclaim God's Word to the congregation. But the daily task of shepherding involves a lot more than showing up on Sunday with some carefully constructed words.

We are constantly assaulted by someone's words. In the course of a day words are used to hurt us, to motivate us to work harder, to give us information we can't use, to peddle things we don't need, and to promise more love than anyone can really offer. After a week of being bombarded with words, no one is going to be overwhelmed on Sunday morning just because the preacher shows up with some more of them. It is for this reason that when God could no longer stand to watch a world that had lost its way, more verbiage didn't shower down from heaven. Rather, we received the Word of God, embodied in the Son.

I have no idea if Jesus was an extrovert, but he sure didn't hang out in tents waiting for people to come to him. There were times, however, when he too grew weary of being controlled by those around him. Sometimes the crowd wanted Jesus to heal or feed them. Sometimes they wanted to make him a king. At other times, they wanted to throw him off a cliff. Eventually they demanded his crucifixion. Because Jesus loved the crowd, he didn't trust them. He didn't trust their agendas for themselves, and he certainly didn't trust their agendas for him. That's because the plans of the crowd never lead to salvation. So Jesus often withdrew to "a lonely place" where his spirit could be renewed as he received the words of his Father.

There are times when I have to be with the noisy crowd. It is my calling, and God doesn't care if I find it tiring. But I'm also called to proclaim God's Word, and that won't come from the crowd. So I can't pretend I belong there. My spiritual home has to be in the quiet places.

ISAAC LOVED ESAU MORE

The father who is most powerful in our lives is the one we have constructed in our memories. Whether or not that father resembles the man who actually raised you is beside the point. It is the father you remember, even if he is somewhat fictional, who retains power over your life. You carry him around with you long after you have left home. He lives in the back of your mind and is free to make comments about any and every activity. He still affirms what is good and harshly judges any performance that falls short of this standard.

Those of us who grew up with loving and patient dads certainly have an edge here. If your father accepted you, it helps you resist the voice inside all of us that constantly says, "You could have done better if you applied yourself." But even if you had Ward Cleaver for a dad, you are still stuck with the judgment that you are not doing enough.

I really believe that most fathers want to do a good job. There are, of course, those who are abusers and those who abandon their responsibilities completely, but they are not the norm. Most of our fathers had good hearts. The problem is not with their intentions, but with their distractions. Like Isaac, they get so focused on creating a blessing, that they forget to *be* the blessing. So the child has to compete with the father's work, recreation, and volunteer work, for the love that the father is trying to demonstrate in being so busy. In the course of this competition for the father's attention, the child learns that there are some things that give the father great delight. Typically these include sacrificing to achieve, delaying gratification, working hard, demonstrating sound character, excelling above peers. Whether or not the child is willing to do these things in order to receive the father's affirmation is another issue. Regardless, he or she still receives these standards as the marks of a life preferred by the father. That is what Esau looks like.

These standards are not only high; they reach the sky. Who ever thinks they've worked hard enough? No matter how well you excel, you could always have tried harder, couldn't you? The reason you ask that question is because your father used to ask it, even if only in subtle ways. He heard the question from his father, who heard it from his father. In order to break the chain along the way someone would have to say that C+ is good enough, and who believes that? "Maybe for others, but not you. You've got potential you aren't using."

I remember gagging when my father said those things to me. I am sure he must have also said plenty of times that he was proud of me, but what I remember most clearly is that I could do better if I just tried harder. Even though I remember hating hearing those little motivational speeches, I find I cannot resist giving them to my own child. I am horrified as the words come out of my own mouth, but I still can't stop it. Striving to look like Esau is such a part of who I am that it is impossible not to pass that inheritance on to my daughter along with all that stuff about unconditional love. "I love you just the way you are, honey, and grades are really not important as long as you are doing your best, but how are you going to improve in chemistry?" Now, what part of that conversation do you suppose she is going to remember later in life? It was as if I told her that I love her potential more than I do her.

Esau is our potential. Jacob is who we really are. Our fathers may want to simply love Jacob, but the sad truth is that they are addicted to Esau. And thus, so are we. If we have the ambition, and Lord knows we do, we will find a way to out-esau Esau. It is the only way to get the father's love. Which means we think it is the only way we will ever love ourselves. That's the way the hustle works.

GRABBING THE BIRTHRIGHT

One day when Jacob was cooking a stew, Esau came in from the field very hungry. It is impossible to know if Jacob set up what happened next or if he just got lucky. Given everything else we know about the Striver, the chances are good he had been waiting for this opportunity for a long time.

"Esau said to Jacob, 'Let me have some of that red stuff, for I am famished! . . .' Jacob said, 'First sell me your birthright.' Esau said, 'I am about to die; of what use is a birthright to me?' Jacob said, 'Swear to me first.' So he swore to him, and sold his birthright to Jacob. Then Jacob gave Esau bread and lentil stew, and he ate and drank, and rose and went his way. Thus Esau despised his birthright."[2]

The birthright entitled Esau to the best portion of his father's inheritance. This wasn't something that Esau earned. It just fell to him because he was born first. Clearly that drove Jacob crazy, and it made matters only worse that Esau had little regard for the birthright. In fact, we are told that he despised it. Why did he trade the inheritance away so easily? It is hard to believe he actually thought he would die if he didn't get Jacob's lentil stew. It is more likely that he thought so little of the birthright that he simply valued it less than a bowl of soup.

The thing that is most striking about this deal is not that Esau was willing to trade his inheritance, but that Jacob was so ready to ask for it. For years he had been thinking about what a lousy deal he was getting as the number two son. He thought about his brother's birthright all the time. It was as if it was a trophy on the family mantle that had a brass plaque on it saying, "Esau's." He walked by it every day. He heard his father speak of it so glowingly at dinner night after night: "Someday, Esau, all of this will be yours." It always filled Jacob with desire.

I don't know a great many rich people who have inherited all of their wealth, but the ones I do know seem different than Esau. They have definite plans for hanging onto all the money. Those of us who have been given little can live with that, because it means that at least they value the things we are trying to get through all our hard work. But if they were to despise the lifestyle we are trying to achieve, it would really undermine our life's mission.

As a veteran of many church squabbles, I have learned that the most effective means of driving someone crazy is to not show up for the fight. People can handle losing a battle, and they can clearly handle winning, but they are actually disappointed when someone quietly walks away. We honor the enemy or the competitor by fighting for what we want. When we just walk away from the struggle we not only disappoint those who wanted to win, we also devalue the "prize."

Most of the great struggles in your life do not have intrinsic value. Rather their value is derived from those whose opinions matter to you. Wasn't your hard work to get an education and a good job influenced by our society's esteem for those things? If you were raised in the Amazon jungles, you would have inherited a different set of struggles based on a different set of social values. Which means the thing for which you are really striving is self-esteem. Ironically, though, you keep trying to get it from the esteem of everyone but yourself.

I believe that after he got the birthright so easily from his brother, Jacob was disappointed. Clearly it didn't satisfy him, because after grabbing his brother's inheritance, Jacob then set his eyes on getting the blessing that was also going to fall to Esau.

The blessing meant more than the birthright. It was the object of all the family's religious affections. From the time that his grandfather Abraham had begun talking to God it was clear that this blessing was the thing that separated their family from all the others of the earth. How many times had Jacob listened as his father told the stories of Abraham receiving a promise from God?

"Go from your country and your kindred and your father's house to the land that I will show you. I will make of you a great nation, and I will bless you and make your name great, so that you will be a blessing. I will bless those who bless you, and the one who curses you I will curse; and in you all the families of the earth shall be blessed."[3]

It is one thing to inherit the family business and wealth. It is quite another to inherit the family's blessing from God. Isaac valued his God more than his life, which he demonstrated as a boy by lying down on Abraham's altar. For Jacob to receive his father's cherished blessing from God would mean that he had at last received his father's heart.

But he had to look like Esau to get it.

GRABBING THE BLESSING

When Isaac had grown old and blind and knew his days on earth were coming to an end, he summoned Esau. It was time to pass the blessing to his favorite son, as Abraham had done to him. He told Esau to hunt down wild game and prepare it the way Isaac preferred. Then Esau would receive the coveted blessing.

This doesn't mean that Isaac just wanted one more great meal before he died. He was planning a spiritual meal with Esau and with God. In ancient society sacred events frequently centered on a meal. The participants in these meals were bonded together in a holy fellowship. This was the context for Passover and even Jesus' Last Supper with the disciples. Why do Christians still commune with each other and their God through a sacred meal? It is a way of receiving the blessing. We were created hungry by God. In communion meals we remember that the hunger is satisfied only by a holy fellowship with the Father.

Esau may deserve to come to the blessed table, but we certainly do not. For that reason some avoid communion, thinking they don't deserve to be in a holy fellowship with God. Of course they are right. But that is exactly why they must come. We don't receive grace because we deserve it, but because we need it. Others come to the sacred meal with the Father pretending to be spiritual enough to deserve the blessing. I think this must grieve God even more than those who do not come at all. It's ridiculous to think you deserve a blessing just because you dress up well.

Rebekah, Isaac's wife, overheard his instructions to Esau. She knew this was her chance to help her favorite son, Jacob, grab the blessing. She also knew her husband's appetites and quickly developed her scheme. Then again, perhaps she had also been planning this day for years. She told Jacob to get two young goats from the family's flock and she would prepare them in such a way that the old man would think he was eating wild game. Then Jacob would bring the food into his father's presence and receive the blessing. "But Jacob said to his mother Rebekah, 'Look, my brother Esau is a hairy man, and I am a man of smooth skin. Perhaps my father will feel me, and I shall seem to be mocking him, and bring a curse on myself and not a blessing.'" Rebekah responded by saying, "Let your curse be on me, my son; only obey my word."[4] After preparing the meal, she put Esau's best clothes on Jacob, and took the skins of the goats and placed them on his hands and the back of his neck where her blind husband was most likely to touch Esau.

Jacob went into his father's presence while his brother was still hunting game. Isaac asked him, "Who are you, my son?" Jacob responded, "I am Esau." It took some convincing, and a few more lies about how the Lord had granted him success in the fields, but the deception worked. Isaac gave the blessing of God to Jacob.

This creates a great theological problem. How can the blessings of God be captured through lies and deceit?

It is important to remember that God had already determined to give the blessing to Jacob when he was in his mother's womb. Rebekah isn't taking anything that wasn't already promised. So the problem isn't what this narrative says about our ability to get ahead with cunning and deceit. The problem is what it says about God who allows the blessing to be given to a family that is as dysfunctional and ungodly as this one.

We want to believe that people who are blessed by God look like a blessing. We expect that this blessing comes as a reward to those who live a holy life. And yet this great blessing of Abraham, which was to weave through his descendants as the sacred thread of God's love for all the families of the earth, is now given to a family that is among the most flawed of all the earth. The Bible scandalizes our sense of justice with the persistent notion of God's grace.

This family clearly doesn't look like a blessing. Jacob and Esau have struggled with each other from before the day they were born. Their parents' marriage has been reduced to trying to outwit each other in giving advantages to their favorite sons. By the time the blessing is given, Jacob has become so obsessed with looking like Esau, that he is almost telling his father the truth when he says, "I am Esau." His God-given identity has been lost in the idolatry of his brother, which he learned from his father. He has resented Esau for so long that he has damaged his ability to be himself. That is what resentment does. In the words of novelist Ann Lamott, "Resentment is liking feeding yourself rat poison and then waiting for the rat to die." In stealing the blessing, Jacob has also stolen something pure from himself.

His mother does, in fact, bear the curse she offered to take on as a result of getting what she wanted so badly. Her family will never be the same as a consequence of her sin. The son she loves so much will have to flee home. She now has to live without Jacob and will instead spend the rest of her life with an angry Esau who keeps marrying women he knows she despises. So no, they don't look like a blessing. But they certainly need one because they are sinners. And that is precisely why God blesses us, as well.

BESETTING SIN

Sin is such a powerful word. It evokes all sorts of responses from within us. Some can feel the hurt and anger well up at just the mention of the word. They have worked hard at getting rid of the shame that someone stuck on them, and they vow never to suffer under that judgment again. A few people even question the legitimacy of speaking about sin at all, wondering if it isn't out of place in modern vocabularies. They would rather speak about neurosis or the misdirected affections of the inner child. But in my experience it doesn't really take much effort to get most people to admit that they have sinned. If you ever doubt that, just spend an afternoon watching daytime talk shows.

I was once visited by a respected therapist who wanted to talk about his guilt over an adulterous relationship. He began our appointment by saying, "I have been to three different ministers and all they offered me was poor psychology. I'm just looking for someone who will hear my confession." Actually, good psychology calls for the confession of sin. So does good pastoral care. So does the human heart.

It isn't that we doubt the concept of sin. But we are confused about what constitutes a sin. Since our society keeps changing the false gods we worship, we also keep changing the things we label as sin. When we worshiped the god of success, people considered it a sin to be a failure. When we worshiped the god of self, it was a sin not to be self-actualized even if that meant breaking our commitments, hoarding our money, or forgetting about the public good. Now that we worship at the altars of pluralism and tolerance, the only unforgivable sin is to claim that someone else is wrong. All of this has left us morally confused. But still we know that something is wrong.

In the Old Testament, sin is typically described as rebellion against God. In the Garden of Eden this was a rebellion against our created limitations. In the days of the patriarchs sin meant a rebellion against worshiping God alone. When David was king, it was a sin to rebel against the kingdom of God. The prophets warned the people about rebelling against God's decree to live with justice and righteousness.

The New Testament adds to this concept of rebellion the notion of missing the mark. When Paul says, "For all have sinned and fall short of the glory of God," he is claiming that no matter how hard you tried, you still missed the mark for which your life was designed. But in both Testaments the results of sin are the same—separation from God. Sin has nothing to do with how badly we disappoint the expectations of those around us, and everything to do with how far we wander away from God trying to find our dreams. Desiring to become something greater than we are, we tragically become so much less than we were created to be.

The old pietists used to speak of a besetting sin. What they were referring to was your favorite sin, or the sin which you find to be most addictive. Some temptations to sin are easy for you to resist. But other people will get tripped up by them every time. By contrast, you may find a particular sin irresistible that they easily avoid.

My first car had a serious alignment problem. The tires were bent on leading the car to the right. If I didn't compensate by constantly pulling the steering wheel to the left, I would end up in the ditch. Your besetting sin refers to your alignment problem, to the particular thing that will send your life into the ditch if you don't compensate for it. Typically these besetting sins are shared among a family, which is where we learn them. Our parents can only pass on what they know.

Deceit was a besetting sin for Jacob's family. One time a famine developed in the land where his family was living. So Isaac moved everyone to Gerar, an area under the control of the Philistines. When he saw that the men of that region were impressed by the beauty of Rebekah, he told them that she was his sister. Now where did Isaac learn that? From his father Abraham, who did the same thing with his wife Sarah when they were in Egypt during a famine. It just so happened that Rebekah's brother Laban was something of a deceiver himself, which later became obvious to Jacob when he was given the wrong daughter to be his wife. So Rebekah was continuing a family tradition when she deceived her husband by dressing Jacob to look like his brother. For the rest of his life Jacob would be tempted to try to get out of every difficult situation with deceit as well. Near the end of his life he discovered that his own sons had learned the same lesson when they lied to him about the fate of Joseph. This is what the Bible means when it claims the sins of the fathers are visited upon the sons and the grandsons.

The oddball in Jacob's family is Esau, who never told a lie recorded in Scripture. It is striking that the one who was most truthful was passed over in the blessing from God. When Isaac tried to claim his wife was his sister, it was Abimelech, the Philistine king, who told him to repent and tell the truth. Pharaoh did the same thing when Abraham committed this sin. Frequently in the Bible, those who are outside the blessing from God have higher morals than those who are blessed. Again, this is evidence that the blessing flows only from the grace of God.

If there is any condition to receiving the blessing, it is not that we are the only people who live by the truth. To the contrary, God's blessing comes as salvation to those who have built their lives upon so many half-truths and non-truths that they no longer know how to see the truth. They have been blinded by their own deceptions and cannot find God. As Jesus said, "The well have no need of a physician." None of the disciples followed Jesus because they saw that he was the truth. They followed only because he called them. In fact, the people who were impressed by Jesus and applied to be his disciples were consistently turned away.

There are so many good organizations in Washington that exist to do really good things. They fight hunger, poverty, crime, illiteracy, disease, and all manner of injustice. For them, the enemy is always external. They go out from their organizations into the world around them to fight evil. That is what distinguishes them from the church. We too have a mission into the world, but that is not where we begin the battle against evil. Our battle begins within the church, and more to the point, within the heart of every member of the church. To use the language of the Reformers, the church is not a school for saints. It is a hospital for sinners where we come to find healing for our sin-sick souls.

The only way you get this healing is through confession. In confession you simply tell the truth once again. Only then can you hear God's truth which claims that his forgiveness is stronger than your sin. His persistent grace can even keep your besetting sin from driving your life into the ditch—again.

The problem with this is that apart from worship you are really not trained to be a confessor. You are trained to be a good manager. So it is easier, you think, to manage sin than to confess it. But the only way you can manage sin is through more sin. After Jacob's first lie to his father he had to keep telling him more lies before he could get the blessing. Then he had to run from home. Then he had to make a deal with Esau. Then, then, then. The hole just kept getting deeper. The only way out is to tell the truth.

YOUR REAL FATHER

It is terrifying to confront the truth that you are Jacob when you have spent so many years successfully pretending to be Esau. But to be a successful liar should terrify us even more than the truth does.

When you do confess the truth, you are always brought back to Jesus Christ who is "the way, the truth, and the life." In telling the truth about yourself, you discover the truth of a merciful Savior who is waiting to bring you home to the Real Father who loves you for being Jacob.

In discovering your Real Father, you find that the sins of the earthly father are redeemed. Since you cannot know yourself apart from your father, it is impossible to find hope simply by fleeing the home in which you were raised. Hope comes only from fleeing to the Real Father who created you and who alone can remind you of who you really are. But that means that your image of the heavenly Father must also be redeemed. Until you shed the false ideas you have about God that were given to you by the model of the earthly father, you will never be free to be yourself. Since your earthly father gave you life, a name, provision for needs, and rules for your conduct, at a very early age he set your impression of God. No matter how benevolent your dad was, he still gave you a limited and flawed understanding of the heavenly Father. That is one of the things from which Jesus saves you.

Until your image of the Father is redeemed, you will never be able to make the changes in your life that you are desperate to make. If you are struggling with being too judgmental, you will have to discover the merciful Father in heaven before you will be free to be merciful yourself. If you are struggling to find joy in your life, you will have to discover the laughter from heaven before you will be able to smile again. And if you are struggling to find hope for a life that appears to be stuck, you will first have to see a God who has a future filled with hope before you will find the hopeful future. That is because the problems you find in your life are directly related to problems in your image of the heavenly Father.

Until you find the truth about God, you will never find the truth about yourself.

THREE

LEAVING HOME

May [God] give you the blessing of Abraham, to you and to your offspring with you, so that you may take possession of the land where you now live as an alien.

GENESIS 28:4

Home is not just the place where you keep your stuff and collect your mail. It is the place where your life ought to be lived. It's where you know you belong, where sanctuary is found, and memories are created. Home has little to do with the new dining-room furniture, and everything to do with the old kitchen table.

You can spend most of your life searching for home. Even if you can find it, you can't buy it. Home is a gift or, more to the point, a blessing. It may takes years in a place before it becomes home. Or you can be at home the moment you arrive. You'll know when you're there because you are no longer a stranger. At least, not for a while.

You'll never find a home you get to keep. You can only borrow it for a time.

PARADISE LOST

Have you ever gone back to take a look at the house where you were raised? Usually the place looks a lot smaller than you remember. The grass needs to be cut. Your mother's beautifully carved flower beds are overgrown with weeds. The big old tree

41

that you used to think was a ladder to heaven is gone. A window shutter is dangling by one hinge. The porch where your date kissed you for the first time is littered with hastily discarded bikes, and the whole place is in desperate need of paint.

A whole series of emotions runs through you. Part of you wants to jump from the car and bang on the door of the house to tell the people who now live there that this is a special place and they ought to take care of it. Instead, you curse yourself for coming, drive away, and vow never to come back. As you leave, you start to wonder what you were expecting. You knew they weren't going to put a brass plaque on the porch announcing that this was where so many memories were created for you. But you had hoped that whatever it was that made the place special would continue to exist there. After staring at the house that now appears so different from what you remember, it is clear that the special thing no longer resides there. Blessings don't convey when property is sold. Thomas Wolfe was right. You really can't go home again.

Even if the house is still in good shape, even if your parents still live in it, the experience of trying to return home is frustrating. It is not what you remembered. The house may not have changed. But the home has. At least for you. Having left that home to look for a place of your own, you can't walk back into it and feel like you still belong there. This is a wonderful discovery for those who have mostly painful memories of that home. They are finally free of the place and are delighted to have escaped. But it is a sad discovery for those who would love to come back to the only place where they remember being blessed.

After seminary, I served as the college pastor on the staff of a large congregation. That gave me the opportunity to care for students when they made this discovery about leaving home. Usually, by the time the students finished college, it was clear that they were also graduating from home. Even if they stayed at home for a while after school, they were not at home. The parents know it. The adult child really knows it.

I found that a family's first glimpse of this loss was the hardest. It happened often during the Thanksgiving break of the freshman year. The student has been in another world for only a couple of months, but that is all it takes. They don't realize this until they walk back into the house and for the first time feel something strange about the place. It doesn't occur to them that they are the ones who are now estranged, and that the only thing that has really changed is their own hearts. The bedroom, that hallowed ground, where clothes were strewn on the floor in just the right places, and whose walls were decorated with the sacred icons of a teenager's culture, just isn't the same. One freshman returned from his vacation at home to tell me that his mother had turned his room into a sewing room!

Some parents try to move more slowly with this transition and leave the room alone. It doesn't really matter. Even if it hasn't been touched by the parents, the blessing has still left the room. The posters no longer tell the student's story in life. The furniture feels childish. The same kid who used to be able to spend an entire day in that room now can't wait to get away and go out with friends. That's all because when you are no longer a child you have to start searching for your own home.

This search will take up the remainder of your life. For a while you may have a place that feels like home, but it's only temporary. Before long the cool apartment had to be left for a house, which in time had to be left for a bigger house, or a new house in a different city. In life's later years the grand old family house, where so many memories were stored, is left for another apartment, and eventually a nursing "home." In every place the home was more than geography. It was a whole collection of experiences and relationships that defined a life. The thing that is hard about moving is not leaving the house, but saying good-bye to a life that was known as we venture out into great uncertainty.

ON THE RUN

A day came when Jacob knew he had to leave the beloved tents of his parents where he had spent his life. That began a pattern for the rest of his life. Jacob was always leaving one home for another. At one point he even tried to return to the home of his parents, but that didn't work for him anymore than it does for us. So on he moved to another place, and the running continued until the day he died.

Like Jacob, we too find that once we leave our parents' home, the running never really stops. Even if we don't change addresses that often we continue to move pretty fast through jobs, relationships, and dreams. We are constantly on the run. For several reasons:

We Are Afraid

Esau was furious when he discovered Jacob had deceived their father and stolen the blessing. "Now Esau hated Jacob because of the blessing with which his father had blessed him, and Esau said to himself, 'The days of mourning for my father are approaching; then I will kill my brother Jacob.'"[1] Whenever Esau discovers that you were pretending to be him, he will do all that he can to destroy your career, your reputation, your relationships, and the home that you have built. He will find a hundred different ways to tell you that you don't belong there anymore and had best be running along. And so you do.

When Rebekah discovered that Esau wanted to kill his brother, she didn't say, "Well, that can't happen. God has promised to bless Jacob." Instead, she feared for his life and got Jacob frightened enough to run away to her brother Laban's home in the distant city of Haran.

Fear is very contagious. It is our worst social disease. Although we live in the most secure time in history, in the most secure of nations, we still have so much fear. Our sociologists are having a field day trying to get behind the great success of industries that sell security in our homes and cars. New housing developments are being constructed all over the country that are surrounded by high walls with guarded gates, as if we were living in the Middle Ages.

Every time I visit my doctor he gives me another pill to take, just in case. "Take an aspirin every day," he says. "It may prevent heart disease. Take one of these vitamins. It may prevent cancer." I always take them, because he has hooked into my fear of what *may* happen.

We feel as if something or someone is lurking out there trying to get us. Which means that we are essentially afraid of the dark. We don't know how or when it is going to happen, but we have heard so many frightening stories from people like Rebekah that we doubt the blessing will protect us. So we run. We run from the city to the suburbs. We run from the suburb we are in to a better one. We run to the drugstore, to the health spa, and to church. We are thinking that if we live well, eat well, and pray hard, then maybe we will be safe.

One of the most beautiful suburbs around Washington is the village of Potomac where the houses typically cost over a million dollars. Not long ago a family who lived there was terrorized by a painter they hired. He slipped into the house in the middle of the day and murdered the father and daughters who were inside. The news of this event was on the front page of the *Washington Post* for over a week. It sent terror through not only the wealthy residents of Potomac but also through the middle-class residents who live in less affluent areas. If you are not even safe in the secure, beautifully manicured villages, then where do you go to find safety? Children are murdered on the inner-city streets routinely in Washington. Reports of that usually appear on the third or fourth page of the Metro section. But if a family is killed in a "safe" community, then that is big news because it means we are all vulnerable.

So we run to buy a better alarm system, we get a dog, we refuse to help stranded motorists, and worst of all, we run away from those whose color of skin or background is different from

ours. We have all heard the term "scared stiff." But in my experience, when people get frightened they are not paralyzed by the
fear. Rather it is then that they run like crazy. It doesn't matter
where they run or what they try next, if they are really terrified
they turn the pace of life up to level ten. That is how we tend to
get lost—running when we are afraid.

It isn't just the physical violence that we fear. Even more we
fear the violence that is done to our dreams about family, marriage, and vocation. When things are not good at work, we work
harder to prove that we are indispensable. When things are not
good in our marriages, we run into another relationship, or we
spend more time at work where affirmation is easier to find. Since
that only makes things worse at home, we simply throw ourselves
more into these affairs with work and other loves. By the time we
realize we are running in the wrong direction, we have lost the
things that matter the most in life. It is hard to hold onto blessings
while we are running.

We Feel Like Frauds

A friend, who is a pastor in an expensive community on the
West Coast, spent all of his money buying a small but pricey home
when he moved there. When it came to transportation all he could
afford was a beat-up old Volkswagen that could barely make it up
the hills, while all the expensive luxury cars raced by him. The
worst thing about his old clunker was that it had a nasty habit of
talking to him. He could swear that every time he started the
engine he heard it say, "Failure!" It insisted on reminding him how
much better everyone else was doing. Finally the day came when
he had scraped together enough money to buy a new car. It wasn't
anything excessive, but it was brand-new. To his horror he discovered that the new car could talk as well. Now when he starts
the engine he hears it say, "Fraud!"

Even when we achieve the level of success that we think will
make us blessed, we are haunted by the voice from within that

says, "Fraud. What are you doing in Esau's car, in Esau's house, in Esau's job?" We keep dreading the day that people discover we are just pretending. We are just dressing up to look like Esau. Maybe blind old Isaac was fooled by the goatskin we taped to our neck and hands, but we know the truth about ourselves. So we start running to another place, where we are not known and where we can start over without our history getting in the way.

I am in terror of the day at church that someone stands up in the middle of a sermon, points a finger at me, and yells out, "This guy is just a chump! He doesn't know what he's talking about. Can't you see he is just dressing up in a robe to look like a pastor? I say we all just go to brunch." I fear that not because the chances are great that it may happen, but because every time I put on the clerical robe and stole I wonder if I'm dressing up to look like someone I am not. Then I start thinking that the place where I belong is back on the wrong side of the railroad tracks, working my old job at the all-night gas station.

We live in a society that makes it incredibly easy to show up in a new place with a new identity. We move easily and often. When we arrive at the new place we can present ourselves as whoever we want to be, and we are free to interpret our histories however we choose. Employers even seem to prefer that. You promote a familiar person to a new position in the company and you have a lot of questions to answer. You hire someone nobody knows from the Land of Oz, and everyone assumes that person must be an expert. As one personnel director told me, it is a lot easier to answer the question "Who is he?" than "Why him?"

What adult wants to maintain the identity he or she had as a child? Remember those awful nicknames, the clumsy looks and huge mistakes? It's too much familiarity. That is one of the reasons why we left home in the first place. We can't pull off the image to which we aspire around people who watched us grow up. Not even Jesus could make that work when he returned to Nazareth. When I return to my hometown, nobody there spends a lot of time looking at my business card. It has too many degrees and titles on it—nothing more than wool I offer for their eyes. They know who I am. That's why I don't live there.

Eventually, however, the wool starts falling off, and it becomes obvious that we are just Jacob no matter where we have roamed. Do we consider that the people around us might be thrilled with Jacob? Few of us are willing to give them a chance to find out.

We Are Tired of Being Victims

After a while, you get tired of reacting to things you cannot control. Although it meant leaving the home Jacob dreamed of inheriting, it is striking that he agreed to run away. Perhaps that is because at least part of him was fed up with life in Beersheba where he always got the short end of everything. Now that he had grabbed hold of his brother's birthright and his father's blessing, the last thing Jacob was going to do was let Esau take it all away.

It is fascinating that at a time in which we are so preoccupied with the rights and freedoms of the individual we are also allowing our lives to be so determined by the "they" who are to blame for our problems. *They* are not like you. *They* will hurt you. *They* will take what you have. *They* have done it to others. It is only a matter of time before *they* do it to you as well. I know this sounds paranoid, but just because you're paranoid doesn't mean *they* really aren't out to get you. So you keep running from them, whoever *they* are.

Every day we confront more opportunities than any people on earth have ever known, but at night we lie awake in bed and wonder where life is going. It is as if we feel our lives are being planned by forces and people we cannot control. We are left feeling like victims.

We see this in the church a great deal. Many of our older members have experienced so many losses in life. They have lost their spouse to a premature death. Their grown children have moved far away to a place where they are busy with their own families and careers. Their doctor of twenty years retired and, at a time when they have more health concerns than ever before, they are stuck in an HMO where some kid fresh out of medical school is assigned to them. They notice that younger people speak to them in ways that feign honor but actually resemble the way someone speaks to a child. Then they get a new pastor who is younger than their own children. So when I make what I think is a minor change in the worship bulletin, why am I surprised to get a nuclear reaction by these who have endured so many unwanted changes? What they are actually trying to say to me is, "Not the church too! It is the last sanctuary I have from all the things that are being taken away."

Even these older members, I have discovered, are good runners. They keep trying to run back to the past, where they remember having so much more control over their lives. Whether those memories are accurate or not is unimportant. The past the elderly remember was so much better, mostly because it offers more control over what *"they"* could do to them.

It is not just the elderly who are tired of being victims, however. We all live with the frustration because we all experience the volatility of our lives. The effect of this is to consume our attention with our own anxieties to the point where we have precious little energy left to care for others. I don't think people lack compassion because they are indifferent to the needs of the world around them. I think we have just become exhausted with ourselves.

Contemporary historians have traced a fundamental shift in our understanding of freedom since the second world war. Freedom used to mean that we were free to work together for the common good. We were free from tyranny and free to control the forces that govern our lives together. But in recent years we have become too battered by the world to still work for the common good. Our families break apart, sometimes despite a great deal of effort to keep them together. The company can downsize and throw you and your twenty years of service right on the street. At a stoplight someone can rip you out of your car and drive away with it. Bring someone home one night to take away the loneliness, and you can wake up to a disease that will slowly suck away your life. It feels like the world is broken and can't be fixed. Despairing that it is possible to improve society, we run to our own lives and do whatever we can to fix them no matter whom it hurts. So now freedom has come to mean not that we are free to serve, but that we are free to do what we want to run from our fears. But a collection of victims each running away from the common good does not make for a free society. What it makes is more victims.

People are not victims just because bad things happen to them. They aren't even victims because they suffer greatly. Suffering is an inevitable part of our lives. Those who are committed to following Jesus have learned that he was serious when he told us to pick up our crosses and follow him. He was also serious when he promised to give us a new life on the other side of our losses. It is hard to perceive the risen Jesus Christ, or his disciples who were martyred for their faith, as victims. Every one of them entered suffering with a sense of holy expectation that they too would discover a new life after their cross.

People become victims only when their goal is to avoid suffering. Since this goal is unobtainable, it isn't long before they discover that someone or something has kept them from a pain-free life. At that point, rather than look for the redemptive use of this suffering, the victim is stuck only with the realization that life is not what he or she expected it to be. Being a victim is a choice. It is a choice to waste your suffering.

We Are Restless

Having spent so much of our lives longing for what we do not have, we cannot be satisfied with the place where we are, no matter how badly we wanted to get there. That is because yearning is more a part of who we are than is having the things for which we yearn. Our society has taught us well how to achieve and acquire, but it has not taught us how to enjoy what we have. So no matter how wonderful the new town or the new job or the new home is, as soon as the new wears off we find ourselves already starting to look around.

No one really enjoys running through life. Relocating is especially difficult. It's expensive. And your family goes crazy every time you announce that you are about to venture off again. But you are addicted. You have to find the blessing, and clearly it is not here. You'll never be at home until you find it. So call Bekins, you've got another job in another part of the country that is really going to make you happy. This time you are going to find home. You've just got to make one more move.

If the circumstances of your life prevent you from physically moving, you can still run from one relationship, job, or passion to another. At least once a week some volunteer in the church calls me to say that he or she is overextended and just has to drop out of a committee, ministry, or mission in the community. I don't really have any choice but to oblige and say, "Well, don't worry. We'll find someone else." But I have noticed over the years that it usually isn't long before that same person is once again overextended with different commitments. Then I know to expect another phone call when we will again recite the same dialogue.

We conduct life as a dance on the borders of a dark and irreversible burnout. We keep jam-packed DayTimers close to our side as if they are the modern equivalent of the six-shooter from the old cowboy movies. They make us feel powerful, and if anyone asks for an appointment, we whip out those weapons and say, "Well, I don't know. Let's see if I have any time free. When? Oh no, I couldn't possibly do it by then." We even like to look busy. Who wants to hear from someone, "You look well rested." No, what we want to hear is, "Say, you look tired. You must be really busy." Busy is good. It means we are running hard. It means we are doing all we can to find a blessing before someone sounds the buzzer and life is over.

Christians tend to believe that in finding Jesus Christ as their Savior, they will be freed from searching. That makes for effective evangelistic marketing, but it just isn't true. Even those of us who have sincerely embraced the salvation offered through a personal relationship with Jesus as Lord and Savior still have to deal with our restless hearts. It isn't that we are looking for more of a Savior than Jesus. But we find that his salvation does not exempt us from still searching for the blessed home, now known as his kingdom. Jesus will keep inviting us to leave the places where we would prefer to stay, and to let go of the things we would prefer to keep. It is the only way we can receive more of the kingdom where he alone is Lord. So not only does following Jesus not exempt us from a restless heart, it actually creates some of the restlessness.

The hardest thing to let go of is our grasp of Jesus himself. When Mary Magdalene discovered that the man who she thought was a cemetery gardener was her risen Savior, she called him "teacher" and reached out to him. But Jesus said the strangest thing. "Do not hold on to me."[2] This is not my favorite part of the Easter story. If I was writing this scene, I would have a big tearful embrace followed by Jesus saying, "Go get the others and tell them that I'm back. We're going home to Galilee to settle down and live happily ever after." My guess is that is what Mary would have preferred as well. But Jesus didn't say that. He said, "Don't hold onto me." The Christian life is a never-ending process of losing the Jesus we were holding only to discover a more unmanageable form of him. Mary thought she had captured him in a safe expectation by making him her teacher. In reality that was just another tomb. And Jesus just won't stay in a tomb.

Our image of Jesus illustrates what we need hope to look like. But there comes a time when that image needs to die because there is more to Jesus than we know. The Easter story is about encountering a risen Savior with whom we are not at home. Not yet. After the resurrection, things do not return to normal. There is no normal. There is no ordinary. A risen Savior is loose in the world. To follow him is always to be searching for something more. We want more of his salvation, more of his kingdom, and a whole lot more of him. But that means we have to get pretty good at letting go of the image of Jesus to which we once were clinging. So even the best disciples of Christ are still restless.

Rather than running to the next available relationship, job, city, or life-changing experience, it is much more helpful simply to spend time with our restless hearts. What does it mean that you are not at home? Why is it that after all these years, and all those changes, you still haven't found what you are looking for? When Christians start asking those questions it will typically thrust them into prayer. The prayer will direct their attention to God, who is the one who made us restless.

SPIRITUALITY EN ROUTE

It is actually rather amazing how much movement there is in the Bible. In both the Old and New Testaments people are constantly en route. Sometimes they ran away from God. Frequently they ran toward God, following the calling that invited them to leave home and move to another place. Even those who began their journey by running from God soon discovered they hadn't gone far before finding themselves back in the Savior's arms once again. You can't be in any kind of serious drama with God and not find yourself on the move.

Very few people in the Bible got their relationship with God straightened out while staying at home. They were not open to the intervention of a Savior until they left the security of the life they knew. Typically it is on the journey from the former place to the new place that faith is born.

I am amazed that when Jesus called Peter and Andrew, they immediately left their nets and followed him. Then he called James and John, and again we are told, "immediately they left the boat and their father, and followed him."[3] These men were leaving not only their jobs and their families, but their homes. In doing that they were leaving behind the identities they once knew. In order to follow Jesus you have to leave something behind. Whatever it is that Jesus is calling you to leave, that thing is your most cherished source of identity. It is the thing that you are really good at and the thing that you have worked hard to build. Jesus invites you to leave that, not because it was necessarily bad, but because you will never be free to receive the salvation of God until you let go of the home to which you were once clinging.

We would all like to see exactly where Jesus is going to lead us before we leave the places where we have grown comfortable. But as the disciples knew, there is something too compelling about Jesus. We cannot see him for who he is, much less follow him, and still be concerned with such things as certainty.

Along the way in their journey, the disciples discovered that they were actually journeying with God. At the point where they make that discovery, we start to witness the conversion in their lives. Conversion is not simply a theological formula for insuring that we are going to heaven when we die. Of course, it is that, but it is also so much more. It is the discovery of God's painful, beautiful, ongoing creativity in our lives which we receive only by following the Savior.

It was that sacred creativity that invited Abraham and Sarah to leave everything and venture out into an unknown future with God. With their move the pattern of God's dealing with the covenant people was set. Isaac and Jacob were constantly on the move. Later it was the Hebrews who were always moving. When the people felt settled in the nation of Israel, that was when they got into the most trouble. So they wound up in exile, where their faith was again restored.

The Gospels portray Jesus constantly on the move, and the most wonderful things happened to people as they encountered him en route to another place. The book of Acts begins with the Holy Spirit blowing the disciples out of the Upper Room at Pentecost so they could move out into the world with the good news of salvation. And the Epistles all describe the life of a new church that was on the move toward the new kingdom.

Through all this movement we are witnesses of our own conversion—the fearful process of becoming a new creation—along the way.

Receiving that sacred creativity is what we mean by the term "spiritual." The longing for spirituality can be found in most every period of history, but sometimes it is felt acutely. Clearly, we are now living in one of those eras. Spirituality is very much in vogue today. It used to be that if you mentioned spirituality at a dinner party, you would never be invited back. Now if you bring up the subject you are the focus of everyone's attention. Spirituality is in the movies, in contemporary literature, and it is a natural part of the conversations at the office. It's a new age.

This new spirituality that is so popular, however, is not the same thing that the men and women of the Bible discovered by leaving home and beginning a frightening journey with God. It is devoid of anything resembling cost, risk, or "losing your life to find it." Rather, it offers a quasi-gnostic escape from the harsh world. Its secret insights, borrowed haphazardly from Eastern religions and ancient mystery cults, are peddled in shelves and shelves of books. Pick your topic: angels, astrology, reincarnation, Celestine prophecies, and even recipes for cooking spiritual food. It all promises to help you transcend the limitations of this life in a more peaceful realm. All you have to do is buy a book.

It isn't hard to get cynical about new age spirituality. But it is more useful to see it for what it really is—a longing for God. A human being is by definition a longing for God, and when we find nothing sacred in the places where we are, we will listen to anyone who has a hope for where God may be found, no matter how bizarre it may sound.

One of the great illusions of our day is that if we can just find a little spirituality, we will be able to cope with our lousy jobs, our relationships that are less than we had dreamed, and our bodies that are not working as well as they once did. As Henri Nouwen said, all of that assumes spirituality is little more than a place in the corner of the boxing ring where we go to catch our breath, get our wounds treated and our courage restored, so we can enter the fray again.

Biblical spirituality is not a way of being reassured. It doesn't settle for helping you cope with how it is. It transforms you and your part of the world. All you have to do is leave everything and follow the Savior.

FOUR

REHEARSING THE DREAM

Know that I am with you and will keep you wherever you go, and will bring you back to this land; for I will not leave you until I have done what I have promised you.

GENESIS 28:15

You have not been abandoned to wander through your life in search of a blessing. The blessing will find you if you just stop running. You are reminded of this when your desperate journey is interrupted long enough to hear the Word of God. That interruption is called worship.

Worship is the ladder between heaven and earth. Angels descend it to tell you the most amazing news! God will give the blessing to you. You hear this news every week in church, but do you really believe it? Or do you, like Jacob, leave worship, thanking God for the nice experience and then continue to run in the wrong direction?

WHY DO SOME FIND HOPE?

During Holy Week of 1997, thirty-nine members of a cult named Heaven's Gate committed suicide in a community outside San Diego. Their belief was that through this death they would shed their "containers" and follow a comet to immortality. The story was well covered in the media, with lots of articles on the background of the leader and various members. It was so well covered, that eventually the coverage itself became something of a story. Why were we all so fascinated by these deaths? Editorials and columnists began to wonder if these suicides were only an extreme form of a desperation many of us recognize within ourselves. A lot of us are tired of looking for a blessing in this world. We may not be ready to join a cult and commit mass suicide, but we do recognize the desperation.

Several members of the cult made videos just before they killed themselves. One woman looked into the camera and said, "Maybe they are crazy for all I know. But I don't have any choice but to go for it, because I have been on this planet for thirty-one years, and there is nothing here for me."[1] With so many precious years of life ahead of her, she concluded that there was nothing good on earth—no blessing to be found.

The same week that we were all reading about these deaths, I had dinner with a friend who is a chaplain at Arlington National Cemetery. As you can imagine, he gets to a lot of funerals, and he hears a lot of stories about how people die. As we discussed the Heaven's Gate phenomena over dinner, the chaplain began to describe how another man, whom he had just buried, died. This man was told that his cancer was advanced and that he had less than a year to live. Being a very methodical career military officer, he sat down with a yellow pad of paper to make a list of all the things he wanted to accomplish before he died. He stared at that pad. And stared at it. Hours later he couldn't think of a single thing to write down. He had enjoyed life so much because he had received so many blessings. So now he was ready to die as he had lived, with open hands and an open heart.

As I prepared the Easter sermon that year, I was struck by these two people who knew they were about to die. What was it that the man with cancer had found that the healthy young woman didn't have? They both lived on the same planet and faced the same obstacles and opportunities in life. Clearly the difference between them isn't that one of them had an easier life, because the contentment was found in the one whose life was slowly sucked away by a painful disease while the healthy young woman died shaking her fist at the world.

I believe strongly that the difference between these two lives has everything to do with that message I was proclaiming on Easter. In the words of the apostle Paul, "If Christ has not been raised from the dead, then our proclamation has been in vain, and your faith is in vain."[2] Our hope, he goes on to say, is not just for life on this earth. Our hope is also for heaven, which isn't just at the end of life after we die, but is above us throughout our life on earth. Our ability to live with hope for today is directly related to our vision of heaven above us. Hope comes not from grabbing everything we can on earth before we die, and it certainly doesn't come from shedding our "containers" in frustration with a planet that offers so little; rather, hope comes from seeing the ladder that connects you to God in heaven, the God from whom all blessings flow.

DREAMS THAT WAKE YOU UP

Jacob was exhausted, discouraged, and frightened by the recent events of his life. Trying to hustle a blessing had resulted only in having to flee the home he had desperately wanted to inherit. He was now on the run to the home of his uncle in Haran, where he planned to hide out for a while. Fatigued from running, Jacob came to a place where he decided to stop because the sun had set. Then he fell asleep.

As a pastor, I see that a lot. People start out pursuing great dreams, but the sun sets before they arrive. Most of the people in my congregation are not living lives that are in shambles, but they haven't exactly reached all their dreams, either. At the point where they realize they aren't going to make it, they start to develop coping mechanisms. Some drink a little more heavily. Others tolerate vaguely dissatisfying relationships and jobs by distracting themselves with new toys that will be amusing for a while. They buy things they don't really need, with money they don't really have, to impress people they don't really like. It's all just a way of falling asleep. When you are unhappy with how life is turning out, when it seems like you aren't going to make it to Haran, when you think your dreams will not come true, it's better to be asleep than be too aware of all this disappointment.

The only good thing about falling asleep is that you aren't running. That makes it easier to receive a few sacred dreams from God. While Jacob was sleeping, he dreamed that a great ladder appeared between heaven and earth. The angels of God were ascending and descending the ladder. And God said to Jacob,

> I am the LORD, the God of Abraham your father and the God of Isaac; the land on which you lie I will give to you and your offspring; and your offspring shall be like the dust of the earth. . . . Know that I am with you and will keep you wherever you go, and will bring you back to this land; for I will not leave you until I have done what I promised you.[3]

Then Jacob woke from his dream, saying "Surely the LORD is in this place. . . . This is none other than the house of God, and this is the gate of heaven."[4] Heaven's gate is found not by searching the earth for a blessing. No, that method always leads to despising life on earth. The gate of heaven is found in worship, where we see the ladder from heaven that angels use to carry blessings down to us.

Before this night, Jacob had been dreaming that if only he could climb the ladder of birthrights and family privileges then he could pull a blessing down from heaven. He climbed far, but he couldn't make the dream come true. It is awful to spend so much of life doing whatever it takes to get up the ladder, only to discover that your ladder is leaning up against the wrong building. You have used up too many years only to get to a place that hasn't made you as happy as you thought it would. Perhaps you are chasing the wrong dream.

PEERING BENEATH THE SURFACE

Most people are familiar with the old song, "We Are Climbing Jacob's Ladder." But notice that according to Scripture, Jacob is never on the ladder. It's the angels of God who are climbing up and down. Jacob's place is on earth, where he receives the blessings that descend from heaven. Receiving is so hard for this striver, and it is hard for us as well. But we can't climb up into heaven and grab a blessing. All we can do is receive one.

Worship is the means by which we learn how to see the blessings we have received. It gives us the vision to peer beyond the appearances of things to their true reality. Sometimes at the door of the sanctuary after a Sunday worship service, someone will say, "Well, pastor, that was great. But now it's time to return to the real world." I am usually gracious when I hear that, but every bone and muscle within me wants to reach out, grab that person by the lapels, and say, "Don't you get it? This was the most real thing you will do all week. Now it is time to return to a world that is so blind to the presence of heaven that it will constantly lie, claiming that you're on your own through life." But I don't say that. I usually just shake the hand, chuckle, and say, "Yes. Yes." Maybe that's because I don't want to scare people away. Maybe it's because I know that come Monday, I'll have my own doubts about living under heaven. It is a hard thing to see when you are swimming in the middle of that thing everyone else calls reality.

Growing up near the beaches of Long Island, I learned early on not to be tricked by the surface currents of the ocean when I went swimming. If you just watch the Dixie cups that are floating past you on the water's surface (these were not the nicest beaches) you may think that the current is pulling you one way, while all along there is a strong undercurrent that is pulling in the opposite direction. Your survival in the water is dependent on being aware of what you cannot see—the undercurrent. Worship is the only way that our vertical perspective gets restored. It allows us to look

up and see the power of God who is at work even underneath the
events of our lives in ways that we cannot see. You've got to have
that vision, because on the surface of things, there are plenty of
reasons to be afraid. And there are plenty of reasons to have false
hopes. All of them will tempt you to swim like crazy in the wrong
direction.

One of the main reasons people get discouraged with their
lives is that they assume life is only a matter of what they see. "It's
just another day at work," someone thinks. "It's just another fight
with my spouse, just like all of the ones that preceded this one and
all the ones that will follow." They can't see any possibility for
change.

Children, by contrast, never assume things are the way they
seem. That is why Jesus kept blessing them, saying we can only
come to his kingdom as a child. Any kid knows that the world is
full of mystery. The ugly duckling could be a swan. The unwanted
stepsister could become the princess. The frog may actually be a
prince. You don't know. You'll have to kiss him to find out. And
children believe they can grow up to become anything they want
to be, because the future is a wonderfully mysterious blank slate.
Unfortunately, when we do grow up, we become so obsessed with
making a living that we starve the grace and mystery out of our
lives.

What a strange term for humans to use—making a living.
Only the God of heaven and earth makes a living, and the promise
is that your life is still being made. You are on the road to a future
God has prepared, and along the way there is more delicious mystery to be encountered.

But you've got to wake up before you can see the mystery.

FINDING YOUR CENTER POLE

The famous historian of religion, Mircea Eliade, claimed that
many ancient peoples constructed their homes by driving a great
stake into the ground, and then building the home around a cen-

ter pole. That pole symbolized the center of the world and the heavens around them. It was their *axis mundi*, or their ladder to heaven. It gave their homes a sense of order and purpose. When disasters would strike, they rushed to the center pole where heaven and earth were held together.

For the followers of Jesus, the empty cross is the great center pole that ties heaven to earth. When disaster strikes, only that cross offers perspective and understanding. The word *disaster* literally means away from the stars and heavens. When you have lost your job, or when the lab report comes back with bad news, or when your marriage is in serious trouble, it feels like the earth has moved away from heaven. It is a disaster. Where are you going to go when that happens? Are you going to run around more quickly? That won't help in a disaster. The only hope is to go back to the empty cross, where you can always find the risen Savior waiting with all of the mysterious hope of heaven.

It is hard to find this center pole when we are imitating the Striver. That is one of the reasons God created the Sabbath for us. The Sabbath is not an opportunity to take a day off from your busy life at work so you can be busy at home. The literal meaning of Sabbath in the Hebrew is "Stop it. Quit." Give it a rest, and be still for a moment.

The reason God commanded us to observe the Sabbath is because when we are still, two things happen. The first is that we confront the truth about ourselves. The second is that we can then encounter the deeper truth from God's Word. In the first act we are forced to look around us to become humbled by our limitations, failures, and fears. In the second we are invited to look up and see the merciful Savior, the one in whom heaven and earth still meet in spite of the truth of our sins.

From its beginning, the church celebrated the Sabbath, not on the seventh day like their Jewish ancestors, but on the first day of the week. That is because it was on Sunday that Christ was resurrected from the dead. For this reason, every Sunday is a little

Easter. But even if you make it to church on Sundays for worship, it's really not going to be enough to maintain your vision that a mysterious, risen Savior is walking among us. It takes finding a little bit of the Sabbath every day. The reason some of us are disciplining ourselves to maintain a daily devotional life is not because we may find a verse of the Bible that will give us the magic answers to the day's problems. Rather, it is because we are learning that every morning we have to remain still long enough to look up and recover the vertical dimension to our lives.

When I wake up in the morning, I can jump in the shower, grab a cup of coffee, and rush off to work to be productive. Inevitably that will destine me to a day of running. Like Jacob, I will either be running to make something happen, or running away because it didn't happen as it was supposed to. But if sometime in the morning I become still with prayer and the words of God, then it will occur to me that all of the important things have already been accomplished today. The sun came up and the earth stayed on its axis without any help from me. The Psalms remind me of that. I have awakened to a world I did not create to receive a salvation I did not earn. The Gospels make that clear every time I read them. And I need that reminder, because there are so many temptations in the course of the day to be my own savior, which is always, always, a temptation to hurry in the wrong direction.

The only way to resist this overwhelming temptation is to see the true Savior whose work is unfolding before your eyes. But you'll never see the mystery that is before your eyes unless you have begun the day at the empty cross, the center pole, the ladder between heaven and earth.

A VISION OF BEAUTY AND TRUTH

Every time I go to New York City, I try to make time to visit my favorite museum, The Frick Collection. The last time I was there I noticed a young family in front of an Impressionist painting. The mother was patiently trying to teach her daughter how to look at art, while the father sat on a nearby bench reading the *Wall Street Journal*. The mother moved the little girl from one place to another to help her appreciate the painting, but in spite of all this wonderful teaching, the girl appeared to be more interested in the buttons on her coat. Finally, in frustration, the father looked over his newspaper and said, "Liz, it's clear that she just doesn't get it." *She* doesn't get it? In the presence of so much beauty, he is reading the financial pages, and yet the little girl is the one who is judged for not getting it. I wonder how much beauty there is around us every day that we are too distracted to notice. There are a lot of days when I just don't get it either. Our culture isn't a great deal of help.

It is the goal of secular culture to squeeze all the sacredness out of our lives, to preoccupy us with the horizontal perspective, and to teach us to avoid the dangerous highs and lows of life. But life gets pretty uninteresting on the safe, flat planes in the middle. You know people with flat souls. All of the creativity and passion has been sucked out of them. They go to work, pay their bills, and take care of responsibilities, but the spark just isn't there. Day after day, they just show up for life and keep busy with things that don't really matter. They have no passion, imagination, or depth. And they never know how to see the beauty that is right in front of them.

You certainly can't behold the sacred by remaining in the safe flat places, because those are not the places God is found.

So many of the biblical theophanies took place on mountaintops, and if you have ever been on a high mountain peak you know why. You're drawn to climb higher and higher, and yet at the same time you grow more and more afraid. On the peak, where the air is thin and the danger is high, it occurs to you that humans don't belong up here. There is no protection from the winds and the sudden thunderstorms. Your life could be snuffed out in a second. And yet, you keep climbing because something is compelling you to get to the top. That is what it is like to approach the holy. We are irresistibly drawn closer and closer, while all along becoming more and more frightened and more intent on fleeing back to safety. Of course, the view from the top of the mountain is unparalleled. The beauty one beholds there is absolutely overwhelming to the soul. But you can't see the beauty without feeling the fear.

The other place where people often encounter God is in the dark valleys of life. There they discover the loving shepherd who leads them beside the still waters. In either case, whether it is to the terrifying mountaintops or to the dark valleys, worship has to express all of the high drama of walking with God. When Jacob woke from the dream at Bethel, we are told that "he was afraid." I don't how much of our worship today is frightening, but it certainly ought to be. The ancients lived with a much greater sense of the unmanageability of the Sacred One who cannot be domesticated by our elaborate liturgies, our feel-so-good choruses, or our carefully constructed sermons. To find ourselves in the presence of God ought to be frightening. There was a reason why they tied a rope around the ankle of the high priest when he went into the Holy of Holies. You can get creamed trying to worship God. Nothing is safe from the Creator's inclination to redeem and re-create.

And yet, if we want our flat souls restored to life, we have no choice but to return to the terrifying place of worship where we can behold the beauty of God. David once wrote that this experience in worship had become the goal of his life.

> One thing I asked of the LORD,
> that will I seek after:
> to live in the house of the LORD
> all the days of my life,
> to behold the beauty of the LORD,
> and to inquire in his temple.[5]

To dwell in the house of the Lord is a Hebrew euphemism for remaining in a place of worship. Since the great temple was not yet built, it is clear that David was not limiting his aspirations to a particular place or liturgy. Rather, his life's goal was to worship every day of his life in order to behold the beauty of the Lord and to inquire or to seek the truth.

Historically the Roman Catholic church has done a better job of helping those in its pews to behold the beauty of the Lord than it has helping them inquire in his temple. The danger of this, as both Protestant and Catholic reformers made clear, is that beauty apart from truth can never reform our lives. It turns the worshiper into a spectator who is not all that different from the little girl at the museum distracted by her buttons. For this reason the Vatican Councils and theologians of the Catholic church have been restoring an emphasis on the importance of the laity inquiring into the truth of the gospel.

By contrast, the Protestant church has historically done a better job of helping its members inquire into truth than we have of helping them behold the beauty of the Lord. We carry our well-worn study Bibles to church and to small group meetings. We read all the latest Christian literature. We dedicate ourselves to knowing the truth. Obviously this is very important. But we cheat ourselves when we assume the truth is rational and careful, while beauty is passionate, subjective, and extravagant. According to David, beauty is half of what any experience of worship ought to offer. For too long Protestants have sat in sterile sanctuaries, which many even call auditoriums, and listened to sermons that are at best academic discourse and at worst severe pronouncements about the judgment of God. Is it any wonder that so many Protestants are now spiritually hitchhiking on the Catholic and Episcopal roads to spiritual renewal? We are now rediscovering Thomas Merton, Brother Lawrence, and Theresa de Avila. We read more of the writings of the late priest Henri Nouwen than do Catholics. We are finding old priests to be our "spiritual directors" and taking private retreats where we engage in the contradictory practice of being a monk-for-a-day. Why? Because we are hungry for a worship experience that is more than rehearsing the right answers. We want to behold the beauty of God.

In my own congregation, this thirst for beauty has manifested itself in a renewed emphasis upon the sacramental life of the church. The sacraments express the gospel in ways that go far beyond the limitations of the preacher's words.

It is one thing to hear someone say, "I love you." It is another thing to get a kiss. There would be something wrong if you only kissed and never expressed your love with words, just as there would be something wrong if you kept saying, "I love you," but never kissed. One is a way of telling the truth, and the other is a way of embracing the beauty.

In the sermon, I am proclaiming to the congregation the truth about God's great love for them. In offering the sacrament, I am giving them an opportunity to experience God's kiss. We have to have both truth and beauty or our flat souls will never be restored.

Once we do see the beauty of the Lord in worship, we are then able to recognize it through all the common and ordinary routines of our days. In fact, we even begin to receive our own lives as if they were the beautiful artwork of God that is still being created. But that brings us back to mystery, which is always the companion of beauty. The beauty of the Lord that is being portrayed in your life is anything but safe or predictable. It is the difference between Monet and paint-by-number. They both use the same materials, but only one is art. The artist creates from the imagination, taking enormous risks to portray the beauty that is envisioned. There are no numbers to follow in beholding beauty. If you want numbers, go back to the financial pages of the *Journal*. But don't expect it to help with your flat soul.

FROM WORSHIP TO GRATITUDE

Pastors spend a lot of time in hospital waiting rooms. We sit there beside family members who are anxiously hoping for a doctor or nurse to give them some news on the person they love. While we wait, we do whatever we can to pass the time, but mostly what we do in a waiting room is wait.

Like Jacob, reeling in despair and fear at Bethel, those who huddle in these waiting rooms are ready for any visions God wants to give them.

I will never forget the afternoon that I was called to the emergency room where Duane Barney was just rushed after a heart attack. Duane was the chair of the search committee that brought me to the church, and he was my frequent advisor. I depended greatly on his mature spiritual counsel, and I depended even more on his gracious friendship.

When I arrived at the hospital, I found Virginia, his wife, sitting with another member of our church staff. After talking about his condition with the physician, we then prayed, talked to each other, read some Scripture, and then we prayed some more. We made a few phone calls to family members who lived out of town. Then we got to that point where you just sit quietly and wait for some news. We waited for a long time. In life, the waiting is so important because it prepares us for the news that comes not from a doctor, but from the Savior.

After about a half hour, Virginia absentmindedly picked up Duane's DayTimer, which had been given to her by the ambulance driver. As she began to thumb through the pages, a gentle smile emerged on her tear-streaked face. On every page, at the bottom of a full day of appointments, Duane had made a list of things for which he was particularly thankful that day. And at the top of every list was the name Virginia.

Duane did not survive that heart attack, but Virginia did. Knowing that she was so dearly loved made all the difference at the end of Duane's life.

Since that day in the waiting room, I have often wondered what people would learn about me if they picked up my DayTimer. Would they discover that I, like Duane, used each day as an expression of gratitude? Or would they simply see a life that had been crammed into the half-hour slots on each page?

I knew that Duane was a strong advocate of daily personal worship, because he asked me every time he saw me how my devotions were going. What I didn't realize was that after over fifty years of beginning each day in worship, the effect of all that piety was to give Duane a grateful heart. In fact, gratitude became pretty much the defining characteristic of his life. His life wasn't particularly easy or comfortable, but that had nothing to do with the reason for his gratitude. He was grateful, because every day he received a fresh vision of the faithfulness of God in his life.

Jacob concluded his worship experience at Bethel the way many churches respond to hearing the Word of God, by presenting the morning offering. He said to God, "Of all that you give me I will surely give one tenth to you."[6] The most important thing to note about this tithe, as it has come to be called, is that it has nothing to do with the law. It precedes the law by over four hundred years. The first person to make this thank offering was Jacob's grandfather Abraham. Both of them gave the tithe, not because they had to, but because they got to.

Notice that Jacob did not say, "I'll tithe in order to get the blessing." However, that is exactly what the Pharisees were saying by the time Jesus met them. They had turned worship and giving into the law, as if it were a way of pulling blessings down out of heaven. That drove Jesus crazy. Any time that we give in order to get we aren't really giving, we are buying. And if Jacob's life demonstrates anything so far, it is that you cannot buy a blessing, earn a blessing, or make one happen. All you can do is receive one. Even receiving the promise of one in worship can make you so thankful.

So Jacob resolved to give back a tenth of everything God would give to him. Giving a tithe is sometimes presented as the standard for Christians. Others, though, are quick to bristle at this, claiming that Christians are not under the law. "You can't say that we gotta give ten percent," they protest. Then from this low point, the conversation usually digresses even lower into an argument about whether it is ten percent of gross or net income, and does it all go to the church or can it include other ministries. This is usually the point where I start looking around for Jesus to storm in and turn over a table or two. This is not some business deal we have to hammer out. It is an expression of love and thankfulness.

Like Abraham and Jacob before us, tithing is a way of telling God, "This is not the life I had planned. It certainly isn't the life I would have made for myself. It is so much more, because it has come from your hands." So the initial question is not, should we give God ten percent or five percent or twenty-five percent? The initial question is, do you realize that one hundred percent of your blessings have come from God? Has that humbled you with gratitude? Everything that you really value in life did not come because you earned it. Those things came as blessings. If you really believe that, you are going to be thankful. People who are thankful find the heart is so full they're afraid it will burst if they don't give something away.

MAKING DEALS WITH GOD

When God reaffirmed his promise to give Jacob a blessing, there were no conditions attached. The Lord just kept saying, "I will give. . . ." The reasons for this gift can be found only in the mysterious grace of God. Jacob has to do nothing to receive it. But doing nothing is not easy for Jacob. He is sure he has to do something, and that is the only thing that makes it impossible to receive grace.

It is striking that Jacob responded to the unconditional promise of God by making a promise of his own. But there is no grace in Jacob's promise, which is phrased in the conditional language of a deal or contract. "If God will be with me, and will keep me in this way that I go, and will give me bread to eat and clothing to wear, so that I come again to my father's house in peace, then the LORD shall be my God. . . ."[7] God has already promised to give all these things to Jacob. When he woke up, Jacob knew that he must have been dreaming. Still, he considered it a wonderful promise and wanted it to be a dream come true. So he promised that he would worship the Lord as his God, *if* all these things would happen. It sounded like a good deal.

I know about making deals with God. I go through several every day. I make deals about my family, my work, my health, and anything else that I value. I even make deals for God to get me out of committee meetings early. Essentially, what I am offering is that I will trust God in all these areas of my life—if they turn out the way I want them to. That is exactly what trust is not. It doesn't take faith to believe in a God who gives us what we want, when we want it. Faith is a choice to trust simply because God is trustworthy. That's asking a lot.

On Sunday morning, when I am lost in the splendor of worship, it is not hard to believe in the dream. But later in the week, when I am confronted with so many reasons to doubt that God will bless me, it seems like the dream was nothing more than wishful thinking. We live in a world that believes in the conditional. *If* we perform well, *then* we are rewarded. In a hundred different ways we receive that message every day. So for God simply to give us a blessing, well, we have our doubts about that.

The primary reason for our doubts, however, is not that our world knows so little about grace, but because we don't really want God to just give us anything. The truth of the matter is that we believe that we do deserve something from God. Maybe, we are not perfect, but we are not the worst specimen of humanity. We can be loyal, hardworking, worshiping subjects, who can do a lot of good. By rights, we think we deserve to be treated as faithful servants who work hard for our Lord at considerable sacrifice. We hate the thought that we come to the bargaining table with nothing to offer.

Well, we do come to the table with something. We have more sin in our lives than any of us want to admit. So when it comes to God, getting what we deserve is the last thing we want.

FIVE

STRUGGLING WITH LOVE

Now Laban had two daughters; the name of the elder
was Leah, and the name of the younger was Rachel.
Leah's eyes were lovely, and Rachel was graceful and
beautiful. Jacob loved Rachel.

GENESIS 29:16–18

After you fell in love, it wasn't long before you realized that
this person was not going to meet all of your needs—not to mention your expectations. Even in good and healthy relationships this
is true. In fact, the way relationships become good and healthy is
when we free them from having to provide what only God can
give us. Love is a blessing in our lives only when we receive it as
a surprising gift, and never when we make it the fulfillment of our
dreams.

SEEING WHAT YOU'VE GOT

Karl and Jan had been members of our church for less than a
year. They immediately threw themselves into the life of the
church, signing up for several committees and ministries. One
night, during a mission committee meeting at the church, Karl
had a massive heart attack and died. In a moment, Jan's life completely changed.

She was in shock, of course, for the first several months. As
she and I talked our way through these early stages of grief, she

wondered if she would ever feel anything other than agony. But after a long time, she did begin to speak more about the blessing it was just to have her husband in her life. She didn't miss the places they went together or the work they accomplished as partners. She just missed Karl. He was the blessing.

Then one Sunday, she saw a young couple having a small argument in the church parking lot. She couldn't tell exactly what they were fighting about, but she knew it couldn't be important. Like every couple, she and Karl had had plenty of these little spats. They all seemed so ridiculous now. It made her crazy to watch this couple. The next week she told me she was tempted to run up to them and say, "Cut it out! Don't waste time on this. Do you realize what you've got? It could all be gone tomorrow."

I have never forgotten that question: "Do you realize what you've got?" When I think about how many nights I've spent at committee meetings instead of being home with my family, the only honest answer is no. I don't realize what I've got. I sure don't think about the fact that someday, maybe tomorrow, I'll have to give it back.

There is no question that you have received blessings. The question is, can you see them in the flawed people God has given you? Of course, the blessings won't be hard to see after they're gone, but if you want to enjoy your relationships, you'll have to look beyond the flaws to find the blessings.

THE TROPHY WIFE

As soon as Jacob arrived in Haran where his uncle Laban lived, he saw Laban's daughter Rachel out in the fields with her father's sheep. It was pretty much love at first sight for Jacob, who was enraptured by Rachel. The moment he saw her, "Jacob kissed Rachel, and wept aloud."[1] It is important to notice that his love had nothing to do with who Rachel was. I think he was in love before he met her. He loved not the woman, but the fantasy he had been chasing for a long time. You can spend a lot of time looking for your fantasy love. Then after you find a person who may fit the bill you can spend even more time trying to make the fantasy come true.

Jacob started working at Laban's sheep farm. His original plan was to stay for only a month, but his love for Rachel changed all of that. So he hammered out a deal with her father: If Jacob worked for seven years, Laban said he would let Jacob marry Rachel.

We are told nothing about those seven years except "they seemed to [Jacob] but a few days because of the love he had for her." But we can imagine how many times he tried to catch a glimpse of Rachel. Every time she pushed that wisp of hair behind her ear, it drove Jacob crazy. You can imagine how many times he passed her a note through her older sister Leah, and how many times he spent the night dreaming about their upcoming marriage. This was going to be the blessing for which he had been striving his whole life. Soon the trophy would be his.

Finally the big day came. We are told they had a huge wedding feast. Then, that night Jacob went into the tent to be with his bride. But in the morning he discovered he was married to the older sister Leah! Jacob was furious. He stormed out of the tent and screamed at Laban, "What is this you have done to me? Did I not serve with you for Rachel? Why then have you deceived me?" Deception, remember, is something of a family problem.

Laban got Jacob calmed down, and explained that in these parts you never marry off the second daughter until the first one is gone. Then Laban came up with another deal. He told Jacob to take a week of honeymoon with Leah, and at the end of that time he would let him marry Rachel. All he had to do was to agree to work another seven years on the farm. So then Jacob married Rachel also, because he loved her more than Leah.

I have noticed at all the weddings I attend that after the bride walks down the aisle and stands next to the groom, they always do the same thing. It is so subtle that most of the congregation misses it, but every couple always does it. They sneak a quick look into each other's eyes. (Apparently they've read this story.) When they do that, I always wonder about the moment that will come not long after the wedding when they will take a much harder look at each other and wake up to the realization this is not exactly the person they thought they were marrying.

Whether you are married or not is beside the point. This is actually a story about love, and the chances are good that you have been in love, or are in love, or will be. So this is really a story about you and your relationships. It's about God's decision to bless you with someone to love, and your struggle to let go of the dream for someone who looked a little different.

THE ONE YOU WANT AND THE ONE YOU HAVE

Whoever it is that you love, that person is both Leah and Rachel. You may love one more than the other, but they are wrapped into the same person. Rachel is the one you love, and you're sure that she will be the blessing to your life. But you can't have Rachel without taking Leah, whom you don't love, and frankly, didn't think you were getting. However, not long after you are together you discover you didn't get just Rachel. You're also very involved with Leah, and you can work for years trying to turn her into Rachel.

Of course, this tension between the love you want and the love you have, is as hard for women as it is men. For all we know, Leah could have preferred Esau, like most everyone else, but her father stuck her with Jacob.

I find that when people fall in love, they are certain that they are in love with Rachel or Esau. Oh, they notice these little flaws in the other person, but at first they are blind to their power. In fact, they don't even think of them as flaws, but as precious little quirks that make the person more colorful. "Well, he's a little sloppy, but it's good not to be uptight about looks." "Well, she does seem awfully dependent on her father, but that will turn my way in time." "Well, he has a little bit of a temper, but I could use a bit more passion in my life." Right.

Maybe when you first fall for this person, you think there is only five percent that bothers you. But a day comes when you're surprised to discover that five percent is taking up most of your energy. So if Rachel is the symbol of the fantasy you want, then most of the time you are not with Rachel. Most of your time is spent trying to improve on Leah. This sets up a tremendous conflict in Leah, who knows she isn't Rachel, just as Jacob knows he isn't Esau. For years they have been trying to improve themselves without success. When someone they love tries to improve them, it only makes them more insecure, guilty, defensive, and thus, even harder to love.

We learn early on in a relationship that our improvement strategies are not working, but we still find them irresistible. Ignoring the biblical teaching that God has already created this person, and has called all creation "good," we attempt to re-create the people we love in our own image of goodness. This has more to do with our own feelings of inadequacies and needs than it does the person we are diligently trying to re-create. What we are really saying is not, "You are not good enough," but "You are not meeting my need to feel good about myself." It is a need that no human being is ever going to meet. This is why so many people today have become relationship consumers, constantly burning out one relationship after another, never being able to settle into the love they have.

Falling in love is not a matter of the will. It is something that just happens to you, like tripping over something. That's why we call it falling. You don't choose to fall in love. But you certainly have to make choices if you are going to stay in love once you realize that you're not in a relationship with your fantasy. You're with Leah.

I NEVER KNEW THAT ABOUT YOU

When the Smiths asked for an appointment to see me "right away," I was not surprised, but I was disappointed. I was the pastor at their wedding two years earlier and had a great investment in their marriage. During the premarital counseling it became clear to me that this relationship was on shaky ground. I tried to persuade them to postpone getting married until some of their serious issues were at least further explored, but it is very rare that a pastor talks anyone out of getting married.

Frequently, I can take one look at an engaged couple in my office and tell that we are not going to get a lot of work done. Often, the last thing they want to talk about is how to make a marriage work. They adore each other! Why would they have to work at marriage? This is why most pastors I know would prefer to do premarital counseling about six months *after* the wedding. By then the adoration has given way to the discovery that they married another flawed human being. It is similar to the discovery that new parents make after they bring their first child home from the hospital. In time, it is clear that this child was not conceived by the Holy Spirit.

For a few months we can adore a teacher or a pastor, a boss or a political leader, and we certainly adore the love of our lives, but eventually it always becomes obvious that this is just another human being, and no human will ever sustain our need to adore someone. That takes someone much more sacred.

I agreed to do the wedding for the Smiths because I have discovered that it is more important for me to be the pastor than to be right about a bad marriage. They were going to get married whether I did the wedding or not, and I wanted to maintain a relationship so they would come back to me when the adoration phase was over. Other pastors strongly disagree with this philosophy, and I highly respect their opinion, but having committed myself to a ministry of grace, I find that I am often walking down the wrong road beside people. It is not unlike God's merciful commitment to stay beside me when I make big mistakes with my own life.

Now, two years later, they were in my office saying they didn't know how they could stay married. We weren't talking fifteen minutes before the anger was all over the place. The hurt that one had caused had consistently been met by hurt from the other, which led to only more hurt. By now, they were trapped in such a complex web of pain that it was hard to get them to look at the real issues that were creating all this hurt. I was getting nowhere. They had refused to see me earlier, in spite of the frequent invitations I had made. They had not taken my advice to see the counselor to whom I had referred them before the wedding. Now, all I could do was watch this marriage unravel. Their argument in my office came to a head when the wife screamed at her husband, "That is so like you—you always do that!" Well, there it is, I thought. After only two years of marriage they have each other all figured out.

Later that evening, I went to a church dinner that some of the older couples in our church have every month. Many of these couples are way past their golden anniversaries. They don't all have terrific marriages, but most of them stand as models of commitment in relationships. During the table conversation at dinner, one of the men made an off-the-cuff remark about how much he always wanted to see Greece before he died. His wife got a bewildered look on her face and said, "I never knew that about you." I couldn't resist smiling.

It is not surprising that the couple that has been happily married for over fifty years is still discovering more mystery in each other. When we have someone figured out, we are in control, and humans are incapable of loving the things we control. That's just one of the reasons why we are not gods. Staying in love means continuing to fall in love, and we can only do that the way we did it the first time when there was so much mystery to discover.

It is actually quite difficult to figure out anything as complex as a human being, and it's impossible if you love this person. That's because God is still creating your lover. St. Augustine claimed that the greatest benefit to marriage is that it commits us to a mystery that is not unlike the mystery of living with a God whose love can withstand our failures and weaknesses. It is only after the commitment has been made, the marriage vows taken, that love can take on the power to keep loving no matter what it discovers.

As we trust in this vow, not only to stay married but to stay in love, we find the freedom to discover more of ourselves and to reveal this mystery to our spouse. One of the great benefits of a healthy marriage is that it helps our individuality to flourish because it creates a safe and accepting environment no matter what is discovered. This is not unlike the way in which our relationship to God molds us into a new creation.

Being the pastor of a church family, I can introduce the different generations to each other. So, naturally, I stayed a while after the church dinner to invite this older couple to meet with the Smiths. They didn't have to become marriage counselors. I just asked them to be themselves around this young couple who were in need of another model of marriage. They were glad to do it, and the Smiths were by then desperate enough to respond to any idea I had. Frankly, I still don't know if their marriage is going to make it, but I do know that our congregation is trying hard to introduce them to mystery, commitment, and, of course, forgiving grace.

LETTING YOURSELF LOVE SOMEONE

It's pretty hard to make yourself love someone. Especially if that someone has disappointed and hurt you or has turned out to be quite different from who you thought he or she was. The Bible calls us to love even our enemies. So the chances are good that God also expects you to truly love Leah or Jacob, or the ex who ran out on you, the parent who was too hurt to love you, the friend who wasn't there for you, or the colleague who betrayed you at work. When you are hurt, the temptation is great to put as much distance between you and the source of your pain as possible. But Jesus is persistent in calling you to return the hurt with love, even though sometimes it seems there is no human way to do that.

That is exactly the right starting point. There is no human way to love this person who has hurt you. You will have to turn to something sacred.

If you choose to be more loving, the first place to turn is not to your strained relationship, but to your God who is love.[2] And what do you find when you turn to God? The message proclaimed on almost every page of the Bible: You have only one Savior. No one else, no matter how made-to-fantasy he or she may first appear, can meet your needs. God alone can save you from loneliness, repair your broken self-esteem, and allow you to stand in the world as one who is good enough.

Until you rest in God's love, you will never be free to love others for the flawed individuals they are. You will constantly be trying to turn them into the Savior, and they will never measure up. Eventually, your needs will become so overwhelming that the people around you will run away for their own protection because you exhaust them so much.

I am constantly struck by the irony that the people who need to be loved the most are the loneliest people I know. Sometimes they will even come to my office to ask, "Why is it that I can't find anyone in this huge church to love me? I'm not necessarily looking for a mate. I would settle for just a true friend. But I feel like I must be wearing some kind of people repellant." If I had enough courage, I would say, "You *are* repelling people. Most of us know that we aren't gods, and we can sense the yearning for one a mile away." But I don't say that. Being addicted to people pleasing, I introduce them to a few other people who I promise will be good friends. Usually it isn't long before they are back to complain about these new friends who have let them down as well.

The problem isn't with them. Or at least that is not the problem that you can do anything about. It is with you. You and your relationship to God. The only way to make progress in your relationship with God is to confess how little progress you're making loving God or anyone else.

Confession is more than a listing of our sins. It's telling the truth. When we confess, we bring to God our broken hearts and broken relationships. We remember the people we've hurt because we were so hurt. Then we discover the most amazing grace, in that God still loves us and for that reason forgives us. Our hearts are filled with so much gratitude the love spills over to our relationships. Which means that if you leave prayer and your heart is not filled with gratitude, even for the Leah or Jacob in your life, then you missed the miracle that was waiting for you in that prayer.

Forgiveness means that God doesn't just love the ninety-five percent of you that is good. All of you is loved, even the five percent that seems so unlovable. That love is what transforms the bad within us and the bad within those we love. You don't get rid of the bad by trying harder. You certainly don't get rid of it by trying to improve the person you love. The only way to change the bad part of the person you love is the same way God is changing your bad part—through love. This is not a love that says, "I will love you in spite of the five percent." It is a love that says, "I will love all of you and will settle for nothing less than all of you, including the flaws. Otherwise the flaws will always stand between us."

That is how people are changed. Nothing else has the power of love. It has little to do with your emotions and nothing to do with technique for getting what you want out of someone else. It has everything to do with receiving grace so you can give it.

SOULS KNIT TOGETHER

We tend to see commitment as a heroic choice to bind ourselves to someone or something. But the Bible speaks about commitment more as a gift. Typically people are not counting on receiving it, and it always molds and shapes their lives.

The friendship between Jonathan and David is a classic illustration of such a gift. Most of the things we have come to believe about how one cultivates a friendship go right out the window on this one. From all appearances, Jonathan and David had no business being friends. They did not spend a lot of time together and didn't have a prayer of being together in the future. They had nothing in common and came from incredibly different back-grounds. Jonathan, the son of the king, received the best education and enjoyed all the powerful privileges of the court. He was an insider. David, by contrast, was educated out in the wilderness with a bunch of animals.

Apparently they met right after David killed Goliath. We are told, "When David had finished speaking to Saul, the soul of Jonathan was bound to the soul of David, and Jonathan loved him as his own soul."[3] When the Old Testament speaks of the soul, it refers to the essence of who we really are. Thus, to claim that the true essence of David was loved by the true essence of Jonathan is saying a lot. It is saying that it is possible to be really known and still be really loved. Most of us do not believe that what Jonathan and David had is possible: Either you can be known or you can be loved. If you really want someone to love you, it's best not to let them get to know all of you, because if they really know you, they certainly won't still love you. We think that way because we have had far too many people reject us once they figured out our flaws. Such conditional love is the antithesis of the biblical understanding of commitment, which frees you to be known, precisely because you are loved.

Lately it has become quite popular to characterize our society as being uninterested in committed relationships of any type and preoccupied with the individual pursuit of happiness. I don't think that is true. At least, it isn't quite true. I think that we are very inter-ested in committed relationships, we just aren't very good at them.

Maybe you remember past hurts too vividly. "Why did I trust?" you ask yourself. "I will never let myself get that hurt again."

Maybe you have a hard time imagining committed relation-ships because you have never seen one. If you didn't grow up watching commitment in your parents' marriage, or if they were not committed to you, then the whole concept seems abstract and unreliable. You can't give what you have never received.

Maybe you are just tired of making commitments to people who always seem to move away. Our world is hard on relationships.

It moves so quickly. Friends, family, colleagues enter our lives only to be whisked away to another place. We write or call for a while, but we know we will eventually lose track of each other.

If commitment is more a gift than a resolve, however, then you can rest in the assurance that the things God binds together do not unravel so easily. When Scripture claims that Jonathan and David's souls were bound, or "knit together" as it says in some translations, it employs the passive voice. Being bound together wasn't something that either of them did; rather, it was something that was done to them. This is true of almost every biblical illustration of commitment. Whether the commitment was to another person, to a nation, the church, or even to God, the people of the Bible never started with these loyalties in mind. But along the way in life they discovered their souls had been knit to these things.

A commitment isn't really something you make, as much as it is something you receive from God. Most of the time, you aren't even asked if you want it. It just comes as a blessing, ready or not, by the grace of God. Like most everything else about God's grace, it will mold and shape your life.

FINDING YOUR PEOPLE

In Albert Camus's story *The Plague*, we are introduced to a devoted doctor who was trapped in the town of Oran after it was quarantined. Every day the doctor did what he could to care for all the people who were dying from the dreaded plague. A visiting journalist by the name of Raymon Rambert was also trapped in the city, but he desperately wanted out. "Why should I die here?" he asked the doctor. "I'm different from the rest of the people. I don't belong here." But he was stuck, and with nothing better to do, he began to accompany the doctor on his rounds. In order to be useful, Rambert did what he could to give the dying some dignity in their last moments. He made a huge difference in the life of a child who broke his heart open.

One day a smuggler offered Rambert a chance to escape from the city, but Rambert surprised the doctor by choosing to stay. "Why would you stay?" the doctor asked. "Your happiness is waiting for you in Paris. You have every right to be happy, and you certainly cannot be happy here." Rambert's response offers the secret to understanding true commitment. "Until now, I have always felt like a stranger in this town, and that I had no concern with you people. But now that I have seen what I have seen, I know that I belong here, whether I want it or not."

I have heard the same thing expressed by relief workers in Gaza, in Bosnia, and in inner-city slums. I've heard civil servants and politicians say it about government. I've heard church members and pastors say it about their congregations. I've even heard people say it about their families. "I know I belong here, whether I want it or not." That is what it means to receive the blessing of a commitment. And that is what it really means to love.

Until you know to whom, or to what, you are committed, you have not begun to live. It has little to do with your plans and everything to do with your responses to the daily unfolding of life. What is happening when mothers wipe little noses and spend their days with car pools and dirty laundry? What is happening in the sacrifices that are made for piano lessons, science fairs, Sunday school, straight teeth, and college tuition? It could be that you are just fulfilling your job as a parent. Or it could be that you are allowing your soul to be knit to a little one. What is happening in the company of friends that you keep? You have walked beside these people for so long that you have begun to assume they will always be there. They won't. When you realize that you can lose these friends, commitment to receive them takes on more meaning. What is happening when a couple struggles together over the decisions of job moves, parenting, or the never-changing challenge of making too little money meet too many bills? It could be that these are the daily opportunities for two people with very different ideas to become truly one flesh.

These are the common, ordinary experiences of life. But when they are all received as blessings, we witness a tapestry of souls being woven together by God. As we come to see the beauty of that tapestry, we get a glimpse of the one who knits us together.

THE MISSING PIECE

One rainy day, while on vacation, my family decided to put a jigsaw puzzle together. It was a huge thing that had a thousand small pieces. It took us the whole day to put it together. Along the way, we joked and laughed a lot. We told stories and had a delightful time simply being a family. But when it got near the end, it was obvious that there was one piece missing. We looked under the table, but it wasn't there. Everyone checked their laps and pockets, but still no luck. That was when I went a little crazy.

I became obsessed with finding the missing piece. I started looking in the strangest places: under the sofa, behind the refrigerator, in the dog's mouth. I made everyone else join me in the quest, as if it were the Holy Grail. I didn't want to hear any more stories or jokes. I sure didn't want to hear anyone start talking about how nice a picture the other 999 pieces made. What about this missing piece? We never found it.

There is not a one of us who has all the pieces put together. That is particularly true in our relationships. There is always something missing in our partner, and there is clearly something missing in our own lives. That forces a choice. Will you find joy simply in the mystery of putting this relationship together, or will you become obsessed with what is missing from the picture?

When the older couples in our congregation who are enjoying their long-term marriages look at each other after so many years, what do they see? The youthful beauty of clear skin and strong lean bodies has given way to wrinkles, chronic aches, and a few extra pounds. The new spouse who could do no wrong now stands in the harsher light of failure and hurt. The hopeful future that once promised tomorrow would always be better has now been eclipsed by the certain knowledge that tomorrow will now bring more medical problems, more loss, and before long, a heartbreaking grief. But that is not what they see when these old lovers look at each other. They are not blind to all of these scratches and flaws, but they have chosen to look instead at all the joy that has come together over the years. They see the beauty of sacrifice, commitment, and the decision to keep forgiving. The vulnerabilities of aging have only made them more precious, more human, more like the people who fell in love long ago.

So the lives of these mature couples are far from over. No matter what the future holds, there is still so much wonderful mystery ahead for them, not because the circumstances of their lives are going to improve, but because they can still receive more of the blessing God has given them in this marriage. They can still choose to love each other, as they have done year after year. And when you can still fall in love, the future is always bright.

Once you choose to receive the flawed people in your life, then you are free to also choose how you will perceive these flaws. There is a strange problem in the Hebrew text when it describes Leah, the wife Jacob had not counted on receiving. Our scholars are not quite sure how to translate the adjective that describes her eyes. Some of our Bibles translate the word as weak, claiming, "Leah had weak eyes."[4] This is how it reads in the New International Version. Other Bibles, such as the New Revised Standard Version translates the adjective as lovely, claiming "Leah had lovely eyes." It has nothing to do with liberal or conservative scholarship. We just can't be sure which is the correct choice since the Hebrew word can be translated either way.

Perhaps the confusion is also inspired by the Holy Spirit. The difference in weak and lovely is significant, but clearly it can be interpreted either way in the text. Leah's eyes could also be interpreted either way by Jacob when he looked at her. He chose to see them as weak, but he could have interpreted them as lovely.

When you look into the eyes of your loved one, long after you have discovered who this person really is, what do you see? The weakness or the love? That is now your choice. God's choice has already been made in giving you this person as a blessing. But you have to decide if you will receive that gift. Choose carefully. This is not just about you and your relationships. It is also a choice about your faith in the Giver.

LEAH: THE BLESSED WIFE

There is a wonderful epilogue to the story of Jacob's relationship to Leah and Rachel. After Jacob had been married to both women for many years, and after his great struggle with receiving God's blessing had come to a climax, he saw the blessing in being married to Leah.

While Jacob was traveling from Bethel to Bethlehem, Rachel died giving birth to Benjamin. Jacob simply buried her in a grave along the way and then continued his journey. It was as if he was finally able to leave behind the trophy wife. When Leah died, however, Jacob had her buried in the family plot with Abraham and Sarah, Isaac and Rebekah, and right next to the place where his own body would finally rest. In the end, Jacob chose to see the lovely eyes.

It takes time to see the blessing that you have been given. More importantly, it takes seeing God in a new way. Until you have lost your dreams wrestling with a God you do not understand, you will never be free to receive the wonderful blessings he is trying to give you.

SIX

STRUGGLING WITH WORK

Jacob said to [Laban], ". . . you had little before I came, and it has increased abundantly; and the LORD has blessed you wherever I turned. But now when shall I provide for my own household also?"

GENESIS 30:29 – 30

After fourteen years on the job, Jacob discovers that he is unhappy in his work. It is not an uncommon discovery. It happens all the time.

You began work thinking that if only you choose the right vocation, you would surely be happy. After a while you discovered that the job wasn't everything you thought, and it was a lot of things you didn't think. The hours are long. The workload is too much. The salary is too little. And your supervisor is the Antichrist. You think about freshening up the résumé, but the ink is still wet from the last time you used it to get the job you now hate. So you start to wonder if you are ever going to find a job that will make you happy.

Perhaps what you are really looking for isn't going to be found in a job. Perhaps you are looking for a blessing.

THE HEART AT ODDS WITH ITSELF

There is a great deal of speculation right now that the American Dream is slipping away. Some people are starting to think that no matter how hard they work, they cannot improve their standard of living. But James Michaels has dismissed this sentiment.

> When you are my age you don't have to ask: Are Americans really materially better off than they were in the recent past? Those of us born in the 1920s and with vivid memories of the Depression simply know how much better things are today . . . If he was fortunate enough to have central heating (less than one third of the population did in 1920), the middle class Dad had to pull himself from bed at 4:00 A.M. on cold winter mornings to unbank the furnace and shovel coal; if he overslept, the pipes froze. But he usually didn't have to rake leaves or shovel snow. Not in the 1930s. That was done by shabby, humble men who knocked at the back door in the mornings asking for a warm meal in return for doing chores.[1]

Michaels goes on to remind us that seventy-five years ago the typical workweek was at least sixty hours, but women worked a lot more than that in the home. The leisure industry didn't exist because no one had leisure. For half of the population the family toilet was a hole in the backyard. Life expectancy was about fifty-four years, which was just as well, because there were few pensions beyond what a gold watch may have brought at a pawnshop.

Seventy-five years ago who would have imagined the advances that have been made for women and minorities, in medicine and technology, or in our incredible standard of living. We still have a long way to go with some of these advances, and we still have to figure out how to insure that these opportunities are available to all the people. But for most of us, the problem is not that the American Dream is slipping away from us. For those of us who have found a way to make the system work, the American Dream is doing just fine. Yet we are not content.

Bill Bennet quoted from Mr. Michaels' article in a speech he gave after he and Senator Sam Nunn were appointed to chair the new National Commission on Civic Renewal. Mr. Bennet concluded his speech by saying, "The troubles we have manifestly have to do not with the pocketbook, not with economics, but with the human heart—the heart at odds with itself."

The heart gets at odds with itself when it is attached to too many things. That is why our lives are so complicated. Some of your heart has been given to work, some to family, church, friends, health, recreation, and maintaining the house. And they all want more than you are giving them. If your heart is like mine, sometimes it feels as if there is a bad committee meeting going on in there. Everyone who showed up at this meeting is a rugged individualist who doesn't really care about the demands of the others who are there. When it comes time for voting on how you will use your time, everyone just screams, "Me! Me! Pick me!" That is usually when we start fantasizing about South Pacific islands. But even if you could pull off a change in your circumstances, you would not find a simpler life. That is because the complexity resides in the heart. When we move, we just bring the complexity with us.

I am getting to the age where some of my friends, who are highly trained professionals, are finding that in spite of their success they are not happy. Some of them are dropping out to simplify their lives. For a while they manage bookstores and 7-Elevens. But after a few years, I have noticed that they tend to own two or three franchises of 7-Eleven, are volunteering very heavily in the community and church, and are still trying to find time for relationships. They are right back where they started, as stressed as ever, because the heart is still at odds with itself.

THE BLESSED SIGNIFICANCE

We are created with a deep yearning to live a significant life. This is not necessarily a big life, but it is a life that, even in some small way, makes a difference. There was a day when people looked to their families and communities for this significance. These were places where we were known and cared about, where we had clear responsibilities and roles to fulfill. But those institutions have changed dramatically in recent years. People move in and out of communities frequently. Family is now something we visit at Christmas, and half our marriages are not working out. So it is not surprising that a lot of us are turning to our work, hoping we will find life's significance in what we do. But I've seen people who are running the country who still don't feel their life has amounted to much. That's because the significance we yearn for is never going to come from what we are doing, no matter how important the work. The only way to feel significant is to believe you are blessed.

Work can never be more than work. It is not a means to getting blessed. It is an expression of gratitude by those who have already found their heart's yearning in the love of God.

So why do we keep working for a blessing at our jobs when only God can give it to us? There are, no doubt, many reasons. Jacob demonstrates a few of them.

We Think the Blessing Comes from Being Necessary.

Jacob took care of the cattle of his employer, Laban. He did a really good job. He knew it, and Laban knew it. Laban counted on him and made it clear to Jacob that he needed him. It feels good, for a while, to be necessary, to be the person that people can count on. It strokes the ego to have the boss put an arm around you and say, "We couldn't make it here without you." But a day came when Jacob realized he was losing his life making Laban a success. He wanted to leave, because he now realized there was no blessing for him in being indispensable. Laban protested, "How will I succeed without you? Do you want a raise? A promotion? You name it." No, what Jacob wanted was a blessing.

I had been in seminary for less than a month when one of my professors said, "Begin each morning in prayer thanking God that you are unnecessary." Those were not easy words for a bunch of aspiring pastors who were convinced they were called by God to make a difference in the church. For almost twenty years I have struggled with that advice. I understand God and creation could get by without me, and that everything I do could certainly be done by someone else. "But surely," I keep thinking, "we are all necessary." The old professor would say, "No. Your life is too important to be necessary." You deserve to be loved.

We can't love things that are necessary, because when they are necessary, we can't make a choice about having them. Love is always a choice. It is a way of ascribing value, of taking the huge risk of placing our hearts in someone's hands. We don't do that because we've got to. We do it because we get to. As a pastor, I am constantly amazed at how we confuse being loved with being necessary. We work so hard at home, at the office, in our volunteering. We settle for being needed when we yearn to be loved.

God didn't have to love you. Your friends and family don't have to love you. The blessing is that they choose to. When you make yourself indispensable, you rob people of the opportunity to love you, and you rob yourself of a blessing that can only be received, never earned.

We Think the Blessing Comes from Being Prosperous.

Jacob made a deal with his employer. He would work for Laban for another year. Afterwards, Laban could keep all of the valuable sheep and goats that were pure and without blemish. Jacob would take all the ones that were "speckled, spotted, and striped."

I have never seen a striped sheep or goat, and apparently they are rare, because Laban thought this was a pretty good deal. But just to make sure, Laban took all the sheep and goats that were already speckled, spotted, and striped, and sent them on a three-day journey away from the other sheep so they couldn't mate with the pure ones. Realizing he had been hustled again by Laban, Jacob came up with a scheme of his own. He took the pure sheep and goats that were left, and made them breed in front of striped poles so they would produce striped babies. I know this technique cannot be found in the *Journal of Modern Agriculture*, but it seemed to work. Pretty soon, all the best sheep were speckled, spotted, and striped, and Jacob was a wealthy man.

It's a strange story. Kind of like the strange things some people do to become prosperous. They make a lot of deals with Laban, their employer. They hustle, they work late hours, they accept promotions that uproot their families, all because Laban promised it would make them successful. They keep jobs they don't like, just to make a little more money. But no matter how much money they collect, it is never enough to buy a blessing. They can buy a house, but not a home. They can buy influence, but not friends. They can buy insurance, but not security. They can buy lots of things, but nothing that they will cherish for long. Laban was just hustling them.

Jesus was very clear about the limited purchasing power of money. One day a man asked him for help in getting more of his family's inheritance. Jesus refused, claiming it is impossible to win a battle over collecting money. You lose even if you win. To illustrate this, Jesus told them a parable about a man who had been blessed by God with abundant crops. Not knowing what to do with all his success, he decided to build new barns to store it all. Then the man said to himself, "Soul, you have ample goods laid up for many years." But God said, "You fool! This very night your life is being demanded of you. And the things you have prepared, whose will they be?"[2] In the words of the musical artist Don Henley, "You don't see no hearses with luggage racks."

You can waste a lot of time building barns. Barn-building is a quantitative approach to life that measures how successful we are by how much we have collected. We don't all collect the same things. It depends on what currency you value. Some value money, others care more about relationships, still others try to store up achievements. But since your barn can never be full enough of the things you care about, you are never a success. Your focus will always be on what is missing. As Jesus cautioned, "One's life does not consist in the abundance of possessions." It consists in the abundance of blessings, which can never be possessed.

We Think the Blessing Will Come from Being Powerful.

We live in a world that has a great deal of power over us. The government has the power to tax our income and regulate our lives. Teachers and employers have the power to make judgments about our work and to determine our futures. People who love us have the power to stop loving us and to break our hearts. Diseases have the power to enter our bodies and cripple our health. Crime has the power to break into our homes and take cherished things away from us.

Day after day, we live under all of these powerful forces. The temptation is great to grab enough power to prevent ourselves from being hurt by others who have so much power. Most people are not addicted to power, but we all fear powerlessness. In no arena of life is the search for more power as obvious as it is at work.

It is significant that the very first sin that was recorded in the Bible was essentially over power. This is not to say that power is sinful. Like money or sex, power is a gift from God that can be used for great good. But also like money or sex, when power is used without humility it becomes abusive and demonic. Today the serpent doesn't say, "Go ahead, eat the fruit and become like God." Now he tempts us by saying, "You better work a little bit harder. You are not doing enough to get the life of your dreams. And you had better hurry up because you aren't getting any younger. Hurry. Hurry. Hurry."

Once a year I have to undergo a medical test that requires me to be off my thyroid replacement medicine. This has the effect of slowing my metabolism down to the point where I am about six inches away from a coma. Or at least it feels like that. I can't drive, work, or even read or write. My wife, Annie, has to ferry me back and forth to the hospital. This annual event creates a fascinating opportunity for me to watch our lives. I am always amazed at how fast the world around me seems to be moving. When we drive on the expressways I am overwhelmed at the speed of the traffic, and usually mention to Annie that any of these cars could jump the median to end our lives forever. She never really appreciates these observations. One morning as we were heading downtown to the hospital, I saw so many people racing up out of an underground subway station on their way to work. To a man who had been artificially slowed down, they looked just like rats running out of a hole in the ground. I mentioned this in my first sermon after recovering from the test. The congregation didn't really appreciate my observations, either.

When the tests are over and I am back on the drugs, I can rejoin the rat race. Then my only real observation is that there is never, never enough time to get all the work done. I am often frustrated that the person in front of me, the staff, or the committees of the church, are not moving fast enough. I keep thinking that if we all just hurried a bit, we could get a lot more done. Then, I am the one who never really appreciates people's observations to slow down.

We actually enjoy confessing that we try too hard, or work too hard, because it is such a forgivable sin in the eyes of those around us. It sounds like a good work ethic that just got a little out of hand, and that's not so bad. But the Bible calls this what it is, namely, sin. It is the idolatry of pretending that we mortals have the power to create the lives of our dreams.

We Think the Blessing Will Come from a Job Title.

I used to believe people when they said things like, "I don't really care about my job title as long as I enjoy the work." But I have been both a pastor and a supervisor too long to still buy that line. I have also spent too much time myself trying to get the job description of my dreams.

Even though we are all hesitant to admit this, it is very important to us to have a good answer when someone asks, "And what do you do?"

The question terrorizes those who think they don't have a very impressive response. It is awful to have to say, "Well, I'm sort of in between jobs right now." Parents who have made the heroic choice to step out of the marketplace long enough to raise a child also dread the question. "Well, I used to be an attorney, but now I'm at home with our children." It isn't that they regret their decision, but they can feel a definite shift in the tone of the conversation after their vocation is known. People's response to discovering that you are a brain surgeon is different from when they discover that you spend all day with runny noses and dirty diapers. Even though my wife works full time, she has always hated the question, "What do you do?" So she usually responds by naively asking, "About what?"

Our society suffers from a fundamental confusion over the relationship of *being* to *doing*. We keep thinking that if we just *do* the right things, we will *be* happy. If we aren't happy, then we ought to *do* something else. The roots of this confusion go back to the days when we were children and our favorite uncle would put us on his lap and ask, "And what do you want to be when you grow up?" We weren't supposed to say, "Happy!" No, we knew we had to say something like "fireman" or "astronaut," which are actually job titles that describe what some people do. So now that we are all grown up and not happy, we assume that we better find a different job title.

The Bible is rather clear in asserting that you never know what to *do* with yourself, without first *being* the blessed creation of God. What you do for a living is important, but it doesn't determine who you are. Only God determines that. Each of us has been created in unique and wondrous ways. Until you find the blessing in that identity, you will never know what you ought to be doing with your time and energy.

THE BLESSED VOCATION

The term "vocation" comes from the Latin word *vocarie* which means calling. God has called you to use your life for a specific vocation. According to the Westminster Catechism, that vocation is not primarily to work, but "to know God and to enjoy him forever." Work is at best only one of several means of fulfilling that calling. Other ways include worship, relationships, community, health, and even recreation. All of these are means to the end of fulfilling your calling to know and enjoy God.

No matter how successful your work is, if it is not helping you know and enjoy God, then you are failing at your true vocation. No matter how great the failure at work, if you have come to depend more on the Savior through this loss, then your work is still succeeding in its real purpose.

In order to keep us clear that work is never more than a means to the end, God often "moves us around." Maybe that is because we pray better when we are on the road.

It is striking that when God called people to go somewhere, they were perfectly happy staying where they were. They had made pretty comfortable quiet lives for themselves as farmers, shepherds, and businesspeople. Similarly when Jesus called his disciples they also were doing just fine as tax collectors and fishermen before they met him. But all of that was just work. The reason people responded to these radical callings, which demanded that they leave behind everything of comfort, was that in their hearts they had always longed to find their true vocation in life. They wanted more than work. They wanted a significant life. So when Jesus came along one day and invited them to drop everything and follow him, they did it! They bet everything on the belief that significance comes not from what you are doing, but from who you are following.

It is also striking that everyone who applied for the job of following Jesus was sent back home. The rich young ruler could not follow because he wasn't willing to pay the cost of trusting only in a Savior. The Gerasene demoniac, the woman at the well, and a blind man were all sent home to proclaim the gospel. Sometimes it's harder to stay home than to follow Jesus to a new place.

The common thread in all of God's callings is that we are sent to a place that Jesus described to Peter as, "where you do not wish to go."[3] In the case of Jonah, that meant going to the enemy. In the case of the apostle Paul, it meant eventually having to return to Jerusalem, even though he preferred to stay with the Gentile churches. What it means for you is going to be known only through prayer and risk. What I can tell you is that it will mean going to or staying in the place where your need for the Savior is most obvious. That is because your calling is not primarily to accomplish something, but to serve God who will always lead you to places where you are in way over your head. No one illustrates this better than Moses.

CHOICES ABOUT YOUR WORK

It started out as just another ordinary day at work. Moses was doing the same thing he had done for years—taking care of his father-in-law's sheep. But then he saw a bush that was on fire, and he heard the voice of God calling his name out of the bush: "Moses. Moses! . . . Remove the sandals from your feet, for the place on which you are standing is holy ground."[4] Day after day, month after month, year in and year out, Moses had probably walked by that bush as he took care of sheep. Now he saw that it was on holy ground, and he was confronting his God in this familiar place. Once he saw that, Moses faced the choice of his life.

Every worship experience forces you to see the familiar differently. That confronts you with the need to make some choices. Even if you have already made these choices, God invites you to make them again—every day—as you head back to work.

Are You Choosing to Work on Holy Ground?

Work is introduced in the very first chapter of the Bible. Humanity was given a job description before we were even taught to worship on the Sabbath. We all have to have some work because we serve a God who works. Creation is portrayed in the Bible as the work of God. Adam's work was to care for that creation. On this side of the Garden, we are called to join in God's work of finding a creation that has lost its way.

That means work is essential to our humanity. This is why it is so devastating when people lose their jobs. It isn't just the money. It is also their created dignity that is jeopardized. But there is a great difference in your created need to work and your job. Your job is not essential to your humanity. In fact, you may think your job is destroying your humanity. Jobs come and go. At best they are a means of fulfilling your blessed need to work. That is a need God designed into your life, and it is a need you will have all your days, even if your work is simply to be gracious to those around you in the retirement home.

There is no limit to the type of jobs that people have. When we add to that the variety of volunteer work that is done, the diversity is even greater. So it's fascinating that we all ask essentially the same questions about work: "Do I really enjoy what I am doing? How do I cope with the stress? What will I do if I lose this job? What do I have to do to get that job? How do I meet all the expectations of me at work, home, and at the church?"

But the question we should be asking is, "Who do I really work for? Who do I choose to make my true employer?" Our culture has taught us to accept too sharp a distinction between secular and sacred ground. God gets Sundays. But at work there is a different lord and a different set of rules and expectations. If we choose to work for God, however, all ground becomes holy. Even the familiar place, beside the same old bush, at the same old desk, where you go day after day, belongs to God.

So no matter who signs your checks, your real job description comes from God's own mission in the world. "I have observed the misery of my people who are in Egypt; I have heard their cry on account of their taskmasters. Indeed, I know their sufferings, and I have come down to deliver them. . . . So come, I will send you to Pharaoh to bring my people, the Israelites, out of Egypt."[5]

Are You Choosing to Accept God's Mission for Your Work?

Now my guess is that, at first when Moses heard God start speaking, he got excited. "I have observed the misery of my people," God said, "and I have come down." Those are incredible words. Those who are enslaved; those who struggle under poverty and violence and oppressive government; those who feel trapped in despair, loneliness, and lifestyles they hate; those who suffer under the taskmasters of diseases that won't go away, grief they cannot escape, and spouses who hurt them, take heart! God has heard the cries of those who weep themselves to sleep night after night because a marriage has lost its intimacy, or a child has left home in anger, or a great dream has fallen apart. God has seen and has heard, and has come down to us.

"Yes," Moses thought, "it is high time God got down here to straighten this out." But the Lord continued: "Moses, you go down to Pharaoh and bring my people out of there." This is where the conversation takes an interesting turn. As God's workers, we are the ones who go down to the inner city, to the neighbor's house, to workplaces, and to the far corners of the earth. We are the ones who go down to the places where people are lost to bring them home to God. And, like Moses, we would rather not go to these places.

Moses said, "Who am I?" Now, that's not a bad question. Who was this shepherd, this runaway fugitive, in the presence of Pharaoh? Who are you and I in the face of a world filled with need? You could easily protest, "I'm not in charge in my office. I'm not capable of making a difference in the lives of others. What right do I have to interfere?" But to our realistic objections, God's only reply is, "What is that in your hand?"

"This?" Moses asked. "It's just a shepherd's staff. It's what I've used all these years to lead sheep through the desert."

"Throw it on the ground, Moses," came the reply. The staff immediately turned into a snake. "Pick it up by the tail."

I don't know much about handling snakes, but I'm sure you aren't supposed to pick them up by the tail. It would take a lot of faith to do that. Of course, that was exactly God's point.

What Is Your Attitude About the Job?

You may not be able to choose the people you work with or the conditions you work under, but you can choose your response to all of it. Viktor Frankl, who survived the Nazi concentration camps, wrote in *Man's Search for Meaning* that the last of all human freedoms is the freedom to choose our response to any circumstance.[6]

You can tell what type of response you have chosen about work by the way you hold things. For Moses, that staff represented something more than being a shepherd. It was the symbol of his struggle with the world. It was what he picked up forty years ago when his early dreams for being a liberator didn't work out, when he got burned-out trying to help, gave up on God's mission, and decided just to get a job. By this stage of life, most of us have picked up a few things in life: a skill, a degree, a child. We've got something going for us. Whatever it is, we hold it pretty tightly. We can even clutch it so tightly that we make a fist to shake at the harsh world and say, "At least I have this going for me! At least I'm good at this! I'm an attorney. I'm a parent. I have an important job." But when we hold these things so tightly, they become our substitute saviors. And they are not good saviors. If you try to turn your job into your savior, it will always become your taskmaster.

This is why we have so much dissatisfaction in our jobs. We expected too much of them. Now they expect too much of us, and we can never perform well enough.

Whenever the disciples were frustrated with Jesus they always went back to their jobs on the fishing boats. They thought that was the thing they could depend on in life. Have you ever noticed that every time we find the disciples fishing, they aren't catching anything? Once they found the Savior with them in their work, however, that was when they began to see miracles. The greatest miracle was not all the fish they caught, but the discovery that the Son of God was with them. Then their jobs of being fishermen were transformed into their true vocation of being fishers of men and women.

People who work for Jesus find themselves choosing a new attitude about success. Is it really success when someone rises to power at the expense of cherished relationships? Is it really success when someone accumulates wealth, but makes no contribution to the world around them? Is it really success when someone spends the first half of life working so hard to get to the top only to spend the rest of life worrying about losing ground? Look instead at Paul's last words to his successor when he told Timothy to take over for him. His time of departure had come. He was done being an apostle. "I have fought the good fight, I have finished the race, I have kept the faith."[7] That is the biblical model of success.

Those who choose to make God their true employer, who choose to make the mission of his Son Jesus Christ their own, who choose no longer to look to their jobs for salvation, they are free to commit themselves to the blessing of receiving God's great work. It began long before them and will continue long after they are gone. For them success is measured not in accomplishments, but in faithfulness; not in the accolades of those around them, but in the joy that wells up from within the soul in hearing, "Well done, good and faithful servant."

PRAYING FOR GOD'S WILL

Most Christians I know want to do what God wants them to do. It is our great hope that we too will join the apostle in ending our days saying that we have run the race well, we have completed the tasks that we have been given by God. The difficulty is that we aren't always certain just what those assigned tasks are. This is not just a challenge for young people. Even those who are well into their careers often wonder if they are still doing what they should be doing with their lives. Pastors are frequently asked,

"What does God want me to be doing now? I am willing to accept that mission for my life, and I want to use the remaining years that I have for sacred purposes in the world, but I just don't know what God's will is for me."

In assisting people as they struggle through this question, I find it helpful to sort through some of the myths that have crept into their minds. The longer they have hung around churches, the more myths there are. The greatest myth is that they will have to go to seminary or a foreign mission field to be of real use to God's coming kingdom.

When I was a boy growing up in the church, I didn't much care for missions month. Every year the church would bring in missionaries who would tell us such exciting stories about their adventures in Africa or other distant places. These were the super-heroes in our church, and the goal was to make us want to become just like them. For some, it worked well. Johnny Burke dedicated his life to foreign missions every year for five years in a row. But I was scared to admit that I didn't really like to travel. So I made my own dedication to God: if I could just stay home and be successful, then I would give my money to Johnny so he could go to the mission field for both of us. Of course, as it turned out, Johnny never left home and I am traveling for the ministry all the time.

The New Testament actually knows no distinction between missionaries or ministers and those who support them. There are all just priests: "You are a chosen race, a royal priesthood, a holy nation, God's own people, in order that you may proclaim the mighty acts of him who called you out of darkness into his marvelous light."[8] Whenever the epistles give a list of the individual spiritual gifts, the list never includes priests as one of the options. Rather, that is included in the lists that describe the whole church, like being salt, light, a city set on a hill. This means that as a description of the church, priesthood belongs to all of us. So the question isn't what do you have to do to become a priest, but what should you do since you are one?

A priest doesn't actually make things happen. Priests wait on God and declare what they see and hear. Our mission is not really about what we do, but about what God is doing. We don't take God to the world, as if the world was void of the Savior's presence before we arrived. We simply stand in the world and talk about the salvation we see breaking in.

How often have you heard a preacher describe the great problems in the world and then ask, "What are you going to do about that?" Some leave church discouraged because the world is broken and they can't fix it. Others, and these are the ones I worry about, leave resolved to take care of things. "Yeah, that makes sense. God needs my help." But it is hard to fix the world. They can't make it right. So they try a little harder. Soon they get angry because their help isn't appreciated. Then they become mean messiahs who try to fulfill the mission of Jesus by hurting people. They are ambulance drivers running over people to get to the accident.

Need does not determine call. God determines call. There is no end to need, but need has not chosen you. God has.

One summer when my brother and I were teenagers living on Long Island, we didn't have a lot to do. Then a great fire broke out in a forest on the eastern end of the island. Wanting to be of help, we grabbed our shovels and drove off toward the fire. As soon as we saw fire, we jumped out of the car and starting putting it out. We had been at it for hours and had made good progress before the fire chief came running up to us, screaming that we were putting out the backfire he had set. Just because there is a fire, that doesn't mean it is your job to put it out. Check with the chief.

TIME FOR PLAN B

So what does God want you to do? After praying, searching the Scriptures, seeking the counsel of others, gaining a clear understanding of your gifts, appreciating what it is that leaves you with joy, and doing all the other homework that we have learned how to do in seeking God's will, you will still need to make a choice. Since there is a choice, there is also a risk, and the risk is that you may make a mistake.

God's mission for your life is too dramatic for a blueprint. Don't assume that all of the details of life have been planned out by God, or you will live in terror of making wrong choices that will destine you only to receiving God's second best for your life. I heard that warning a lot when I was in my church youth group. "Be careful of your choices. God has a wonderful plan that you don't want to miss. Don't settle for second best." I have probably even given that talk to youth groups. But there is no such thing as second best. There is just the often mysterious will of God and people who are trying hard to figure it out as it unfolds along the way.

We need to spend a lot more time developing what I would call a "Theology of Plan B." This is a theological framework that would allow us to say, "I thought I was supposed to do this. But it didn't work. I need Plan B." The Bible is filled with illustrations of people who wanted to do the right thing with their lives. They set off in a particular direction. It didn't work out. So they had to move in a different direction. Moses' first plan was to kill the taskmaster who was beating a slave. David's first plan was to be a shepherd. Jonah's first plan was to go to Tarsus. Jeremiah's first plan was to prevent Jerusalem from falling. Peter's first plan was to prevent Jesus from being crucified. Paul's first plan was to evangelize Jews. All of them had to go to Plan B, which was God's plan from the beginning.

If we don't get our mission right the first time, we're tempted to think that we must not be called by God. That is because we think the number of mistakes we make is the measure of our spirituality. But making mistakes is never condemned in the Bible. What is severely condemned is refusing to take risks in serving God. Remember how severely Jesus rebuked the servant who hid his talent in a hole because he didn't want to lose it? It is one of those "cast him into outer darkness where there is wailing and gnashing of teeth" passages. By contrast, mistakes made by people who are trying to do the right thing can always be redeemed. You may think you've got a lot of wasted time in life, but as Moses, David, Peter, and Paul can tell you, anyone who turns to God discovers that nothing is ever wasted. There is a use for everything.

If God has called you to fulfill a specific mission in this world, then the calling is not going away. You don't have to settle for second best, but you have to get off the hook for being right all the time. We call that hubris. It is one of the deadlier sins.

SEVEN

STRUGGLING WITH OURSELVES

> I am not worthy of the least of all the steadfast love
> and all the faithfulness that you have shown to your
> servant....Yet you have said,"I will surely do you good."
>
> GENESIS 32:10, 12

We are better at getting things than we are at keeping them. It is not hard to get into a relationship, but it takes a lot of work to keep one. It is not hard to commit yourself to a job or a volunteer opportunity, but it takes a lot of work to keep that commitment vibrant and joyful. Our society has trained us well to achieve and acquire, but it hasn't taught us how to enjoy what we have. Usually it isn't long before the new house, the new relationship, or the new job in a new town seems pretty ordinary and routine. Then you realize this latest passion in your life hasn't made you any happier than the other things you've collected. You become unimpressed at the people and the opportunities you have. You start thinking you need to rearrange your life. Maybe you even feel desperate. If that's true, then you don't care who you hurt in your reckless pursuit of happiness. You don't even care if you hurt yourself.

WHY PEOPLE SELF-DESTRUCT

Behind the struggles we have with love and work lies the more profound struggle we have with ourselves and our own choices.

But that does not make the struggle any easier. It actually makes it harder because nothing is as complicated to figure out as yourself. Even the apostle Paul once threw up his hands saying, "I do not understand my own actions. For I do not do what I want, but I do the very thing I hate."[1]

Because the struggle with ourselves is so difficult, most of us try to resolve our inner conflicts by working on the more tangible struggles we are having with the world around us. But no matter how many victories we win out there, they do nothing to bring peace to the battle that is raging within our own hearts. Eventually, the war within causes so much damage that we become desperate to find peace at any cost. We are even prepared to dismantle the life that we have spent so many years futilely trying to save.

I find that it is at this point that people begin to self-destruct. They have affairs with people they don't love. They leave their families and church. They sabotage their own careers. Typically, they don't think they are about to self-destruct. They just start making some big changes in their marriage, their job, or their lifestyle. What never occurs to them is that maybe they need to change their heart.

I understand the search for a new life. Around the church we call that redemption. But new life doesn't come from starting over. It comes from believing that you have been blessed by God. As a pastor, I've watched too many people waste the precious few days they have on this earth impotently desiring. Trying to find happiness in something else, they keep throwing away the blessings they have. Jacob, the Striver, is our enduring illustration of this.

Jacob decided to leave Haran where he had spent the last fifteen years working for his father-in-law, Laban. It took a little bit of scheming, but by the time he left, Jacob had a great deal of wealth, two wives, and eleven sons. But none of it had really made him happy. So now, he is heading for home, the Promised Land, where he thinks he will at last find the blessing for which he has been striving his whole life.

He doesn't get very far before he hears that Esau is heading toward him. Esau, remember, is the reason Jacob left home in the first place. When Jacob learns he is now riding toward him, along with four hundred men, he is terrified! For the last fifteen years Jacob carried that fear in his heart. It never went away, and now his great nightmare is about to come true. Esau is going to kill him.

Fear, I believe, is the fundamental reason why people self-destruct. Something has been chasing them for a long time. Maybe it is a sense of guilt for what they have done. Maybe they feel like an imposter. Maybe they're afraid the years are racing by them, and they will never be happy unless they do something drastic. Maybe they aren't even sure what they fear, but they just think that somebody, somewhere, is trying to take something away from them. They tell themselves they had better act and do it in a hurry. But when we make decisions because we are afraid, that is always when we make the biggest mistakes with life.

I have noticed over the years that people say some of the same things when they are about to make huge mistakes with their lives. Behind each of these announced reasons, however, lies the fear that has plagued their lives for a long time. Seldom do people say that they are afraid. What they usually say is one of the following things:

I've Been Living a Lie.

After years of thinking that they will be happy if they just look happy, they have now decided that the pretense isn't working.

Keeping up the appearances of being happily married or happily employed is exhausting. So is acting like you have faith in God when you don't. As awful as it would be to admit to others that you have been pretending, eventually that doesn't seem as bad as continuing to live with the secret you know about yourself. You're frightened that you'll go crazy if you don't tell the truth, and you know you'll go crazy if you keep trying to believe the lie that you are more than you know you are.

More often we are tempted to believe we are less than we are. The devil once took Jesus to the pinnacle of the temple in Jerusalem and said, "If you are the Son of God, throw yourself down; for it is written, 'He will command his angels concerning you,' and 'On their hands they will bear you up, so that you will not dash your foot against a stone.'"[2] Clearly, the devil is trying to foster some doubt in the mind of Jesus. "If you are the Son of God, the beloved," can lead to "Am I the beloved? How can that be? I'm just a carpenter from Nazareth. Who am I kidding?"

Whenever we find ourselves at the pinnacle in life, inevitably we start asking ourselves questions that are given to us by the devil: "What are you doing up here on the pinnacle? You don't think you are really beloved, do you? Sooner or later it is all going to crash down. Why don't you just jump and get it over with?"

When people are about to jump into a huge mistake, it usually does not help to remind them of the things they will leave behind or to warn them of how far they will fall, because they don't really care about that anymore. They have spent a lot of time climbing up to the pinnacle hoping that they would be loved when they got there. Now they realize it was the devil who took them to the top, and they have grave doubts that they will ever be anyone's beloved.

I'm Successful; I Should Be Happy.

One of the favorite myths of our culture is that if you work hard and achieve your dreams then you will win the prize of being truly happy. The fascinating thing is that almost everyone knows this isn't true, but still so many knock themselves out to become successful at all costs.

It seems that the people who are most susceptible to this myth are those who choose to cope with their fear of being unhappy by working harder. If in the first half of their lives it was fear that drove them to build their careers, by the second half of life that fear will become unbearable. Now they've run out of achievements and accomplishments, which for a while numbed the anxiety. As long as there was another goal before them, they could believe that happiness would come when they achieved it. But after they have met all their goals they have to face the fear that they may never be happy. So now they are desperate, and desperate people tend to do desperate things.

We used to think that of all the great sins, pride was the most tempting. But I'm not so sure that is still true for people in our society. In our day, it seems that the greatest temptation is to despair. Never before have people had so many opportunities, and yet never before have we been stuck in such a malaise of discontentment and restlessness. The suicide rate is at an all-time high, the average tenure in a job is getting shorter and shorter, and we have never been as careless in our relationships. Is this not because we have lost hope that anything good is coming for us? Having arrived at the top and then realizing that the view of our lives isn't as good from there as we thought it would be, we easily succumb to recklessness. People only become reckless when they have lost hope.

Someone Changed the Rules.

Those whose morality is determined by the ever-shifting norms of our society are often dismayed to discover that they have spent the best years of their lives living by standards that are now easily tossed aside. For example, a generation of women were told that if they stayed at home to raise their children and do the ironing then their husbands would provide for them. But when the husband ran off with his twenty-five-year-old secretary, the dutiful wife was left alone without job skills, money, credit, or, most importantly, a loving companion. Now she is afraid to trust anyone because she doesn't want to ever hurt that bad again. Before long, her fear has chased her into a lonely and bitter existence. She self-destructs with the choice to be a victim.

The last generation also began working for major corporations with the implicit deal that if you work hard and devote yourself to the company, it will take care of you. But after seeing too many fifty-five-year-olds downsized out onto the street, few still maintain that illusion. Afraid of losing the job eventually, many choose to jump ship into ill-conceived schemes for self-employment. But when there are no rules or commitments in the workplace and workers are afraid of what their employer might do to them, many take their chances going it alone.

More significantly, if the company or even the government can break their commitment to you, then it is irresistible to wonder why you should maintain your own commitments in life.

I'm So Angry; I Could Never Forgive.

We think that our refusal to forgive the people who hurt us is a way of continuing to hurt them. Actually, it is just another means of self-destructing. Frankly, the people who hurt us can get by in life just fine without our forgiveness. But we will slowly be eaten away by the anger unless we expel it. To forgive means to free, or to let go. Seminary professor Lewis Smedes has written, "When we forgive we set a prisoner free and discover that the prisoner we set free is us."[3]

I find that the people who have a hard time forgiving others frequently are afraid to let go of the hurt. The greater the hurt, the more true this becomes. After a while the hurt becomes so much a part of them, that they wouldn't even know who they are without it. This is why Jesus sometimes asked people, "Do you want to be healed?" To be healed from a hurt that someone has inflicted on you always requires a choice to forgive. Broken hearts don't just improve in time unless we get rid of the diseases they are containing. Healing comes not from outliving our hurt and certainly not from hanging onto it. It takes open-heart surgery. We have to let the Savior remove the bitterness that is taking up so much of our hearts there is little room left for things like love. But it is so frightening to let Jesus remove the anger because we think it is now a point of our lives. So the anger spreads, like a wild cancer, until the heart is too diseased to love.

I Have No Control.

Those who feel overwhelmed by a need for something that is destructive are tempted to think they have no choices, or that their choices are beside the point. All they can do is watch as their lives are slowly destroyed. Typically, the things that overwhelm us don't start out with that kind of power. At the beginning we think that we are controlling our bad habits. But in time, our use for this thing turns into a need for it, which then digresses into it using us.

The alcoholics in our congregation all tell a story that is remarkably similar. At first they were drinking because it was enjoyable. Then they drank because they found it useful. Eventually they drank because they had to. By the time they realized they were addicted, they were afraid to look through sober eyes at the damage they had done to themselves. So they kept drinking. The striking thing is that they all agree they had to hit bottom before realizing that the only choice they could make was to affirm that they were powerless over this addiction. I've often wondered why things had to get so bad before alcoholics call on the Higher Power to help them. Most of them say that it was too frightening to discover that they are powerless, and for that reason addicts keep resisting the truth. But by the time they hit bottom they are getting used to being afraid. Only then can they find the courage to accept help.

The same pattern is found in the lives of those who struggle with addictions to sex, money, power, drugs, or even abusive relationships. It is the fear that drives them to self-destruct. If they are really fortunate, they will get tired of the fear. But by then they have lost everything.

COPING WITH FEAR

There is no limit to the ways that people cope with their fears. Some try running, but they can never run far enough. Others get mean and cynical, but that only makes you less of a human being. Still others just give up, thinking that if they just give in to the thing that terrifies them they will be okay. But you can't make deals with terrorists. Don't expect mercy from whatever it is that makes you afraid.

When we cope, we develop ways of living with things that are wrong, we allow the problem to determine our agenda, and we establish ourselves in a pattern of constantly reacting. So the fear with which we are coping never goes away. It just becomes the bully that continues to extort more and more anxiety from us.

Those of us who identify with Jacob know that our favorite means of coping with fear is to come up with new plans. These are not plans to diligently pursue the will of God, as was discussed in the previous chapter, but plans that assume there is no God. Niels Bohr once said the mark of any profound truth is that the opposite of it is also true. While it is true that we must pursue the will of God by drawing near in prayer and then planning more than once to do the right thing, it is also true that our plans can get us into great trouble if they are motivated by our fear of anything or anyone other than God.

Out of his fear of Esau, Jacob first plans to divide all his wealth into two parts, and then he separates them. That way if Esau destroys what he sees, he'll only get half of the loot. The second thing he does is to pray and cast himself on the mercy of God. In this prayer he reminds the Lord of his promise, "I will surely do you good."[4] Immediately after that prayer, before he even wipes the sand off his knees, Jacob then comes up with yet another plan.

I am tempted to pray like this—to sandwich my prayers for deliverance between a few ideas of my own. That makes prayer simply one more thing to try.

The next plan that Jacob develops is impressive. Rather than let Esau come and destroy everything, Jacob decides to give him what he has. He separates all his livestock and launches a great parade toward Esau. First came 220 goats, followed by 200 sheep. Then came twenty rams, thirty camels, forty cows, ten bulls, and thirty donkeys. He told the servant at the head of the parade to explain to Esau that these are all gifts from his servant Jacob. Then after the livestock, Jacob even sent his family. Leah went first, of course, then Rachel with all the children and servants. His hope was that by the time Esau waded his way through all these gifts that he would no longer be angry at Jacob.

It was quite a plan, but the text tells us that after he had given away everything he had "Jacob was left alone."[5]

That is the problem with most of our plans for dealing with whatever it is that makes us afraid. They leave us forsaken by the very things we were most worried about losing. Those who get married just because they are afraid of being alone, are surprised to find that their marriage has made them even lonelier. Those who work so hard because they are afraid their family may not have enough, are surprised to find their family that has everything—but love—has fallen apart. Those who were afraid their lives were going to be insignificant if they didn't grab some power, are surprised to find out how lonely life is at the top. Those who were afraid of the bully at school or at work, or even at home, and who determined they had to get vicious themselves to survive, are surprised that their anger has made them so lonely.

Most of the deep wounds in life are self-inflicted. That is what fear does.

There is another way. Rather than focusing on the threat around you, focus on your own heart, because that is where your fear resides. Nobody can make you feel anything. When you are afraid, it is because you have chosen to let that feeling overwhelm you. The feeling isn't out there. It is in your heart. You will never vanquish the fear by coping with things out there.

So how do you get rid of the fear in your heart? Look again at Jacob's prayer, at the words from his own lips that he did not really believe. "O Lord, remember your promise to do good to me." It was a promise Jacob had received before he was even born. It was a promise that God had repeated to him when he ran away from home, when he was in exile, and when he returned for home.

It is the same promise that God has made to you. He has repeated it Sunday after Sunday when you sit in the pews of worship. He tries to remind you of it at work and at home. He has written it on almost every page of the Bible. The question is not whether the promise has been made that God will do good to you. The question is, are you listening to the promise, or are you allowing the still, small voice of God's Spirit to be drowned out by the noises that make you afraid in this world?

As the great biblical story continued centuries later, eventually it got so hard to hear the voice of God that his only Son Jesus Christ came to be with us. In his life that Son kept illustrating that God loves you. In his cross and resurrection he proclaimed to all the world that nothing, not even your sins, can separate you from the love of God. If you believe that, if you believe that you don't need to fear God, if you believe that God will do anything, even give the Son, to do good to you, then what in the world are you afraid of?

Jesus, who was so tender and compassionate and tolerant of our many failings, was absolutely unforgiving of those who were afraid. Remember how he responded to those who were afraid to leave home to follow him, to the rich young ruler who was afraid of losing his wealth, and to the disciples who were afraid of the storm at sea? Jesus is so hard on our fears because they are indications that we have not yet received the love of God. "Perfect love casts out fear."[6] Not trying harder. Not running away. Not becoming mean. Only God's love will make you unafraid.

FINDING THE TREASURE

The self-help market has made a great deal of money off of our fear that we are stuck with ourselves. We keep thinking that if we just find the right formula we will at last be happy. So we try the latest fads in health or assertiveness, or in becoming a more effective manager of time, family, and success. But the self-help concept is not really offering help. What these authors are actually peddling is the possibility of changing your life to become the person of your dreams.

Sometimes people come to church hoping that God will do for them what all of the books, seminars, and exercise have failed to do—change them. In our church we don't talk too much about change. We prefer to speak of conversion.

God does not convert you by modifying your behavior through a lot of religious activity. Rather conversion begins with opening your heart to believe the voice from heaven calling you beloved. Only then can you discover what your true identity has been all along. The more of this new life that you receive, the more you discover that it does not look totally strange to you. What it looks like is a purer form of yourself. It is the self you were created to be from the beginning. It is the restoration of the image of God on your life.

The difference is that the self-help market keeps peddling the idea that you will be happy and lovable only if you change your behavior or thinking to become someone else. Conversion lets you discover the work God is doing within the life you already have. It claims that there is a wonderful treasure within your heart that God just loves. Self-help tempts you to climb up to another pinnacle. God invites you deep into your own heart, where the treasure lies.

We find that hard to believe because the treasure is buried beneath lives that look so ordinary and unimpressive on the surface. But that is only because "we have this treasure in clay jars.'"

My mother used to keep two very distinct sets of dishes. One of these resided in the china cabinet. It was pretty special and would only be brought out when important people were coming to dinner. To get caught using the good china for a bowl of Wheaties was close to an unforgivable sin in our house. For the family meals we always used the other set of dishes. Instead of the beautiful cabinet, these dishes were kept in the dish drain by the sink. They included a collection of Corelle Ware with a variety of different patterns on the edges, a couple of plates on permanent loan from the church kitchen, and a wide assortment of scratched glasses bearing the names of the Empire State Building, McDonald's, and the Red Moon Pizzeria.

If you came over to dinner and Mom set the table with the Corelle Ware, it meant you weren't a very impressive dinner guest. But it also meant that you were considered family.

In trying to describe the people of God, Paul compares us not to the good china but to earthen vessels, early church Corelle Ware. The church is like a set of dishes that have been badly battered and yet still contain the treasure of the gospel, the proclamation that you are a beloved member of the family. "We are afflicted in every way, but not crushed; perplexed, but not driven to despair; persecuted, but not forsaken; struck down, but not destroyed."[8]

You can take your place at God's table anytime. You belong there, not because you have become so impressive, but because you and your scratched-up life are beloved.

BELIEVING YOU ARE FORGIVEN

The reason we have so much difficulty believing that we are the beloved of God is that we know too much about ourselves. We are fully aware of what we have done and left undone, and we have great difficulty loving ourselves as a result. So how can God do that? That is why we are so intent on changing ourselves to become more loveable and why we are so ready to destroy ourselves when all these plans fail.

The Bible is rather clear about this. God doesn't love us because we deserve to be loved. The love only comes by the mystery of forgiving grace.

The whole concept of grace is difficult for us, which is particularly unfortunate, since grace is pretty much the fundamental point of the gospel. We can at least take comfort in knowing that the early church had a hard time getting it also. The apostle Paul spent most of his letter to the Romans, and a good portion of his other epistles, trying to explain God's grace. The illustration of how badly we need it is the fact that we can't quite understand it.

Grace is better than getting the job you've always wanted, having Ed McMahon show up at your door with a million dollars, and getting married all on the same day. It is better than the fulfillment of your dreams. It is the fulfillment of God's dreams—your forgiveness.

Grace is God's determination to give us what we need and not what we deserve. It isn't really a difficult concept, but that is not what confuses us. It is the gift that we can't quite accept. Do we really want what we don't deserve? I think that is the hard part. We know that if we accepted this grace it would shake the foundations of our carefully constructed lives. We would have to begin life all over, as if we were born another time, to begin living a passionate dream with this lover God who will clearly do anything to save us. We would even have to lose interest in carefully constructed lives because, well, that may be the most dangerous sin of all.

This returns us to our fears. While strictly forbidding our fear of anything or anyone, the Bible consistently tells us to fear God. Most of us have been subjected to far too many sermons on the frightening judgment of the Almighty who is waiting to clobber everyone who did not lead a holy life. The Scriptures do provide some painfully clear expectations about how we ought to live, but that is not why we should fear God. The primary reason why we fear God is not because of divine judgment, but because of divine love.

The holy Creator of our lives, the God who keeps the sky and stars from falling, the God who holds back the oceans from flooding the earth, the God of heaven and earth, was not content to simply spin the whirling planets. In Jesus Christ that God has come looking for you. This is no ordinary lover you have. This one is going to be hard to control.

Still, we give it our best shot. With an incredible lack of humility, we tell God how this grace ought to be manifested in our lives.

"If you really loved me. . . ." We say that because mystery drives us crazy, but every time we domesticate God into some useful purpose, whatever it is that we then have under our control ceases to be sacred. Soon we realize that what we thought was God was actually our own aspirations written in large letters. It won't satisfy. That is because we were created with a passion to be loved by the Sacred. Ask any happily married couple and they will say that you can't love what you control.

TURNING TO THE CROSS

The extreme biblical illustration of self-destruction is Judas. The reason his life ended so badly was not because he was so bad at sin, but because he was so bad at receiving grace.

Throughout history, the societies of our world have all reserved their greatest judgment for those who commit an act of betrayal. It is a sin against trust that exposes ambivalence, if not malice, at the deepest core of our relationships. Betrayal is a destruction of commitment, a shattering of our loyalty and faith in someone. It has the power to undermine the security of a marriage, a church, or even the nation. It destroys the life not only of the person who is betrayed but also the person who does the betrayal, because treachery severs the relationships that are critical to life. That is why we have always been hard on the traitor Judas and all his contemporary imitators.

We don't know much about Judas. It's clear that Jesus and the other disciples trusted him a great deal. He was their treasurer. Apparently he was sitting next to Jesus at the Last Supper because Jesus said the one who would betray him was "the one who has dipped his hand into the bowl with me."[9] To be sharing a bowl with Jesus meant that Judas was sitting in the place of honor and trust which makes his betrayal all the more painful.

I keep wondering why Judas betrayed Jesus. Was it for the money? Was he just disappointed in Jesus? Or had he never made Jesus the Lord of his own life? When Jesus announced to the disciples that one of them would betray him, they all exclaimed, "Surely not I, *Lord*," except for Judas who said, "Surely not I, *Rabbi*." Was that the problem? Did Judas only see Jesus as his teacher and not his Lord? We don't know for sure. Maybe that is significant. Maybe the important thing to remember is that there are many reasons to betray Jesus.

We are told that Judas betrayed him to the chief priests for thirty pieces of silver. According to Exodus 21:32, that was the exact amount required as payment for killing someone's slave. Did Judas think of Jesus as his slave, as the servant who fulfills expectations? Was that the problem? Maybe. All we know for certain is that when the events of Holy Week turned dark, Judas betrayed his only hope for a Savior.

Could it be that the reason for both our scorn and our curiosity about this man is that we are afraid there is a Judas chromosome within us, a terrible possibility that we too are capable of betrayal? When Jesus claims that one of us will betray him, the fragility of all our relationships is revealed by every disciple saying, "Surely not I." It is as if to say, "I have been worried about that for a long time, but I was sure I had it under control." The sin that is most difficult to forgive in others is the dark one with which we struggle in our own lives. This is particularly true if we have become good at lying to ourselves to the point where we no longer think we have a dark side. No one is as merciless as those who have no mercy on their own evil.

It is important to remember that in Jesus' last hours, none of the disciples were exactly models of faithful commitment. Three times Peter denied ever knowing Jesus. Apparently, John was the only disciple who made it to the cross. After Jesus' death, none of the disciples even attended to his body. At a time when commitment could have cost their lives, all twelve failed. That is what we fear. Sure it is easy to be a disciple now, but we don't yet know about that Judas chromosome. When will it kick in? Since we live with the possibility of betrayal within us, we fear Judas more than we do the cross. The cross is a symbol of heroic self-sacrifice, but Judas is the symbol of the evil within us.

Sooner or later we will betray Jesus and his message, just like all the other followers. We will betray him by not living as a disciple when it could cost us, by the things we say in anger to those who trust us, by the commitments we made that we can no longer keep. There is little question about the inevitability of betraying Jesus. The question is, what will we do after that sin?

When Judas realized the gravity of his actions, he was filled with shame saying, "I have sinned by betraying innocent blood."[10] We are told that Judas even "repented." To repent means to turn. The problem was not that Judas didn't repent, but it was to whom he turned in his sin. In his shame, Judas turned to the chief priests who despised him. He tried to make the sin right by giving back the money, but the priests were too self-righteous to contaminate their treasury with blood money. This was Judas's fatal mistake. He turned to the wrong place. Peter and the other disciples lived with their failure and betrayals until they saw the risen Jesus, who alone could offer them forgiving grace. But according to Judas, there is no forgiveness. There are just your awful mistakes and the inability to make them right. So in despair, Judas went out and hanged himself.

Despair is one of the worst forms of fear. It is being afraid that there is no hope. We succumb to this temptation when we are dominated more with a sense of ourselves, our inadequacies, and our failures, than we are by the presence of a Savior. We despair when we get to the point of realizing that all our best efforts are not going to fix the problems we have created. Like Jacob, even after we have given all we have to give, we still have to face Esau who terrifies us. Like Judas, even after we throw the thirty pieces of silver on the floor, we are still stuck with our guilt.

None of your efforts at managing sin will relieve your guilt. The only thing that will suffice is to turn to the God who is waiting for your confession. Frederick Buechner has written, "To confess your sins to God is not to tell him anything that he doesn't know. Until you confess them, however, they are the abyss between you. When you confess them, they become the bridge."[11]

I am struck by the fact that Judas and Jesus died at the same time. The one was suicide, and the other was sacrifice. Judas's self-destruction illustrates the tragic end of all life that has no hope. Jesus' sacrifice created the possibility of another place to turn, to forgiveness, to redemption, to the passion of a God who still loves us.

Judas's story is about the tragic fall from the heights to the depths. But the greatest tragedy is that he did not turn to the Savior. He was not at the cross to hear Jesus say, "Father, forgive."

EIGHT

STRUGGLING WITH GOD

Jacob was left alone; and a man wrestled with him until daybreak. . . . Then the man said, "You shall no longer be called Jacob, but Israel, for you have striven with God and with humans, and have prevailed."

GENESIS 32:24, 28

Life is not easy. It certainly has moments of great joy, but they are interrupted by grief, sickness, and things that break your heart. A little girl's body is sucked away by leukemia. A man comes home exhausted from work to find a note from his wife saying, "I won't be back." A student flunks an exam in law school that he had to pass. Now he's not going to be an attorney. They're not exactly sure how it happened, but once again life is in the ditch.

After a while you give up so many dreams, you start to wonder where life is heading.

People of faith have always been asked to believe that we are being led to a future filled with hope. But when your life is in the ditch, that's asking a lot. A whole lot. The ditch you could find on your own (and you did). Now you must enter into a deeper struggle, namely the one you have with God, who promised to give you that blessed future. So it is God's credibility that is on the line. And it is with God that you must now contend.

WRESTLING IN THE DARK

Jacob is now at the lowest point in his life. He is frightened, discouraged, and he has lost everything that he spent years collecting, including his wealth, home, job, and even his family. And he is so tired of running. He ran to his uncle Laban to get away from his brother Esau. After he ran away from Laban, the only place he could go was back to Esau, who wanted to kill him for the things he did at home. Now it is all coming down on top of Jacob. There are no more new towns to move to, no more new jobs to start, no more wives to marry, no more chances for self-improvement. Now Jacob is all alone.

Esau and four hundred men are thundering toward Jacob. He is alone for what he fears will be his last night. In the darkest part of the night a "man" comes to Jacob and begins wrestling with him. A lifetime of frustration finally erupted from every muscle and fiber of his body. He's beyond schemes and careful plans. Now there is just the raw sweat and ache of two men locked in conflict. The struggle is intense and long.

At daylight, Jacob was amazed to see that he has been wrestling God.

This fight is the symbol of Jacob's life. He has actually been wrestling with God for a long, long time. His struggle with love and work were caused by his struggle with himself, and he is never going to get that resolved until his struggle with God is over. This night, Jacob finally gets to the core issue. Now that he has lost everything that he strove to gain for himself, he is ready to contend with the One who has been his greatest problem all along— the God who blesses.

This night wrestling is also the symbol of *our* lives. We also believe in the blessing. But on those nights when the losses and heartaches start to pile up, you have to fight to keep believing. Those are the long nights. As long as you can still emerge with faith in the blessing, you have every ability to slog your way through the other struggles of life. But once you lose your belief in the promised blessing, you know you'll slide into a dark and meaningless abyss. So by the time you get around to wrestling God, there is a lot at stake. There is nothing after this struggle. Tonight it is all on the line.

This type of struggle is done only at night, when it is dark and we are tired, spent, and out of resolve. It may be daytime for other people, but not for those who are wrestling God. There isn't even enough light to see that it is really God with whom you are wrestling. By the time you get a glimpse of God's face, the struggle is almost over. That is why Jacob wrestled until daylight when he recognized the face of God. If you can just see God, you know you'll be okay.

When I have had the honor of talking with people who are in the midst of these dark struggles, they often ask, "How long will this go on?" All I can say is, "Until the day breaks." There is nothing anyone can do to make the night shorter. It can't be shorter. You are not done with the struggle until you are done, and it will seem dark and lonely the whole time. It took Jacob his whole life to get ready for this night. Now that it is here, the wrestling will be long and hard.

FAITH THAT WON'T LET GO

This struggle is not a sign of Jacob's lack of faith. Rather it is faith that is creating the problem. This is the struggle of a man who believes in God's promise but who can't see how it is going to happen. His problem is not just with the difficulty of life, but more profoundly, it is with God, who has promised to do good to him. When you watch a child that you raised in a loving home grow up to reject that love, or you discover that you have an awful disease, or you find yourself trapped in a job you hate but cannot leave, those are not just personal problems. When you read in the newspapers about whole nations starving to death, societies suffering under great injustice, and children picking up guns on inner-city streets, those are not just social problems. For people who believe in God's control over life, these are major *spiritual* problems.

If Jacob had no faith, he would simply accept life as a haphazard collection of injustices. But Jacob takes God far too seriously for that. He can't live one more day with the contradictions between his faith and the way life is. He can't fix it on his own. All he can do is grab hold of God and not let go. The man says, "Let me go, for the day is breaking." But Jacob replies, "I will not let you go, unless you bless me."[1]

Would that we had the nerve to pray like this. "God, we have come to you in prayer, because we believe in your promise to bless our marriage. We have tried too long to make a blessing happen, but we have only made it harder to love each other. Now that we have hold of you, we will not let go until you bless us!" That is the gutsy prayer of a couple who takes faith seriously enough to wrestle for its promises.

In the course of this struggle with God, Jacob's hip is thrown out of its socket. What could be worse for a hustler than to be too crippled to run through life? So now he hangs on to God, refusing to let go until he gets his blessing. This is the final position of faith: broken, exhausted, with hands empty enough to cling to God.

Wrestling with God is serious business, and the chances are great that you will get hurt in the process. From all appearances, this wound in Jacob's life was permanent. It was a grace in that it made it very hard for him to keep hustling, but it hurts to be wounded. This stands in contrast to our expectations that God will make us whole and complete. There is nothing in the Bible that promises we will have perfect lives if we only call on God. What is promised is that we can cling to God for a blessing. But that is a dangerous thing to do.

Why does God cripple the people who are just hanging on for a blessing?

FORGIVING GOD

It sounds ludicrous to forgive God. We forgive those who have done something wrong. God, the Bible says, is just in all his dealings with us. God is all-good and all-powerful. But I am a pastor who has learned over the years to recognize anger when I hear it, and there are few things that make us more angry than being hurt. When we are hurt we look for someone to blame. If we are robbed, we can blame the thief. If we lose a job, we can blame the employer. If we are divorced, we can blame the ex or maybe even ourselves. But who do we blame when we get terrible diseases or when floods and great storms tear apart our homes? Who do we blame when a famine leaves Third-World mothers holding dead children? At some point, it gets hard to keep God off the hook for every bad thing that happens. Although we rarely admit it, we can become angry at God for allowing such awful things to occur. Even if our hurts are caused by others, couldn't the almighty Miracle Worker still have prevented our suffering?

In John Updike's novel, *Rabbit Run*, Harry Angstrom comes home one night to discover that his drunken wife has accidentally allowed their baby to drown in the tub. Heartbroken, Harry goes into the bathroom and kneels by the tub. He pulls the stopper out so easily. He groans, "How easy it was, yet with all the strength of heaven and earth, God did nothing. Just that little stopper to lift."[2] I have heard too many good and faithful people express that deep groan that wells up from within the soul. I've felt it myself. While we still believe with our heads that God is not to blame, with our hearts we express deep lament that God has let us suffer awful hurt.

The book of Job is such a relevant narrative because it allows us to tell the truth about how we feel. At the beginning of the story everything is fine for Job. He has a wonderful life filled with wealth, good health, a wonderful family. And he is a righteous man. Then God allows Satan to take everything away from him. One day his children are all killed and his wealth is stolen. Still Job remained faithful to his God. The next day his health falls apart with "loathsome sores from head to toe." Job's wife can't stand it. She encourages him to simply curse God and die. Job resists her advice, but not easily.

He is bothered not just by the devastating losses of his life, but even more by the great theological problem they create. "The arrows of the Almighty are in me ... the terrors of God are arrayed against me.... Therefore I will not restrain my mouth; I will speak in the anguish of my spirit; I will complain in the bitterness of my soul."[3] Through forty painful chapters we hear Job cry out to God asking, "Why? O God, why have you done this?"

Good religious people cannot stand to have other good religious people angry at God. Soon Job's pious, thin-lipped friends came to visit him. They came not to comfort, but to explain. We have such a passion to explain suffering. Perhaps that is because we believe that if we can explain it, we can avoid it. In the end, these explanations are all lacking because they avoid the fundamental issue of the character of God, the one with whom we must wrestle.

Suffering Is a Punishment for Sin.

The logic of this argument is that there must be some reason for the awful things that are happening to you. But you can't blame God, and since you are the only other candidate for responsibility, you must have done something to deserve this.

The Bible makes it clear that God has, at times, chastened us for our sins. That was why Adam and Eve had to leave the Garden. It was why Moses could not enter the Promised Land, and why the Israelites later had to leave it in captivity. In all of those instances the punishment was the result of bad choices people had made. But not all of the calamities biblical people experienced are attributed to either their choices or God's justice. The fact that God sometimes punishes does not mean that all bad things are punishments.

Job did nothing to deserve this much heartache. Neither have the refugees who flee massacres in Africa. Neither have families whose loved ones are killed by drunk drivers. Neither have children who are abused by their parents. When Jesus and the disciples found a man who was born blind, his disciples asked Jesus who sinned here, this man or his parents that he was born blind? Jesus' response makes it clear that they had just asked a really bad question.

Suffering Is God's Way of Sensitizing Us.

Others assert that the purpose of our problems is to leave us more compassionate and tender. Suffering certainly has the capacity to do that. But if suffering is the price we must pay to be compassionate, then the price is too high. What does this explanation say about the character of God? Does God allow young husbands to die early just to make their lonely widows more sensitive to the grieving? Do some people have to starve in order to make me thankful for food?

Nothing is beyond the reach of God's redemption. Something good can come even from suffering. But to say God causes the suffering to make us sensitive is to take the advice of Job's wife. It is to curse the unjust God and die. If God would do awful things to other people just to teach you lessons, then we are all in more trouble than we know. We are better off dead.

Suffering Is the Result of Our Free Will.

This explanation reminds us that God did not intend on life being so painful. Our own choices have caused the world's pain. Thus, the mess is our mess.

The problem with this explanation is that it is helpful only in a very cosmic sense. Job made no choice. No one chooses to have cancer. The people in oppressed countries who do not have homes did not choose for tanks to come and blow them apart. In the book of Job the only ones who are making choices are God and Satan.

Some of the best theological writing on this topic is centered around this explanation. It does provide help with some of the theological issues involved in our suffering. But suffering is not an "issue," it's a personal problem, with names and faces and stories that will break your heart. I have never found such cosmic theology to be much assistance when I go to an emergency room to comfort a mother who is about to fall apart over the bed of her dying child. Am I going to explain free will to her? If an explanation doesn't hold up in the emergency room, it doesn't help.

Suffering Is a Test.

Sometimes it is asserted that through suffering both God and we discover what we are made of. It is true that suffering will do this, and this also has some biblical warrant to it. But not all suffering has the benefit of testing our character. What is the test when an earthquake kills thousands in a Third-World country?

God knew that Job was righteous before his troubles began. God knows us, too, and has to be aware that if there is a test, it is often too hard, and too many of us will fail. A god who is obsessed with testing creatures is not the biblical God of grace.

Suffering Is Simply a Part of Human Life.

This explanation has become increasingly popular in current literature. In very sentimental language it claims that our moments of pain are part of the natural rhythm of life, much like the stark cold of winter that eventually turns to the bright joy of spring. Well, that makes for good Hallmark cards, but how can a baby born with an addiction to crack ever be seen as a natural part of life's rhythms?

If you stay with this explanation, it will not be long before you succumb to the postmodern, nihilistic doubt about whether there is any meaning or direction to life. It is just a random succession of events that can be either painful or joyful, but there is no purpose to them. Eventually, you will begin to have grave doubts about the benefits of having either a god or a life.

FINDING GOD BEYOND THE EXPLANATIONS

Eventually Job got fed up with the explanations of his friends and cried out, "If you would only keep silent, that would be your wisdom!"⁴ When you are really hurting, what you want most of all is not an explanation. You want hope.

As we progress through the story of Job, as we progress through our own suffering, we slowly begin to realize that the question "Why?" is never going to be answered. But it is critical that we ask it, because it is the only way to get to the real question: "Who?" The question "Why?" is a prayer. Whenever we ask, "God, why did you hurt me?" we are always ushered into worship. That reminds us of who we are and who God is.

In a sacred moment God came to Job in a whirlwind and reminded him that as a creature he will never understand God the Creator. Strangely, Job is satisfied with this. "Formerly," Job says, "I had heard of you by the hearing of the ear, but now my eye sees you."⁵

There it is again. It is the exact same experience Jacob had. As soon as both men moved from their beliefs about God to actually encountering a revelation of God, they were transformed from agony to hope. There is no explanation to the suffering, and at this point the circumstances of their lives have not changed a bit. But they don't need an explanation once they have seen God.

Recently a U.S. senator who is a member of our church buried his father. At the funeral his mother fell out of her wheelchair and broke her hip. A blood clot formed a few days later, went to her lungs, and then she too died. The day after his father's funeral, the senator's son was rushed to the hospital with spinal meningitis. This was one of the most important men in the country, but now he was as powerless as every human in the face of losses that can't be stopped. As I spoke to him, I wondered in the back of my mind what I could possibly say. I reached deep into my bag of theological training and pulled up nothing that could possibly explain this. So I just prayed, without too many words. My prayer was that somehow through the tears, this man would eventually see the face of his God. He has no other hope.

We can see God, not just as the Creator who speaks from the whirlwind, but as the God who loves us so much and shares our suffering. Rather than rescuing God with explanations, the New Testament makes the incredible claim that God is found in the company of the suffering. His name is Jesus Christ.

A GLIMPSE OF GLORY FOR THE SUFFERING

The Gospel According to John begins by saying, "In the beginning was the Word.... And the Word became flesh and lived among us, and we have seen his glory, the glory as of a father's only son, full of grace and truth."[6] That is who Jesus is. He is the Word of the God we have had from the beginning.

The term for "lived," or as it is sometimes translated "dwelt," in the Greek is *Skenoun.* It is a derivative of the Hebrew word *Shekinah.* In the Old Testament the high priest went to the Holy of Holies in the Tent of Meeting, or later in the Temple, to encounter the Shekinah glory of God. John is telling us that Jesus Christ has now become the dwelling place between the people and God's glory. That is a dwelling place to which all mortal flesh can come. The ancients thought that only people like Moses or the high priests could get a glimpse of the Shekinah. If ordinary folks like us ever saw God they knew they would die, because it meant God was coming to judge their sins. The message of the Word in Jesus is that God has come not to judge you, but to save you.

That is the miracle that we celebrate every Christmas Eve. In the birth of Jesus we saw the glory of God, and it didn't kill us. God is not out to get us. That is not what the suffering of our lives was ever about. Our sins are known, but God still loves us too much to abandon us to the darkness, even the darkness of our own making. That is the glory that we behold. In becoming flesh, God has taken on our defiled, broken, darkened lives.

In his life and ministry, Jesus insisted on identifying with the outcasts, the sinners, and all who were in need of a Savior. In the agony of the cross, the Son of God even took on our great night wrestling with his Father. Among his last words was the question why. "Father, why have you forsaken me?" With those words he demonstrated the high cost of grace by taking on the "god-forsakenness" of us all. Again, we then have to move from our question "Why?" to "Who?" Any struggle that begins by calling God to account for abandoning us in our suffering can only end by looking to the cross to see who is with us even in our abandonment.

The eminent psychotherapist Carl Jung was fond of telling the story of the rabbi who was asked, "Why was God revealed to people so often in ancient times, but today, no one ever sees God?" The rabbi responded, "Because now, no one can bow low enough to see God." We keep thinking that we will get a vision of God if we climb up. But that is how Jacob wasted the first part of his life. The best perspective on God comes from the bottom places of life, in your lonely dark night when you feel your abandonment. You are not alone. Jesus Christ is there with you, which means God is found in your great struggle against suffering.

That is not even the best news. The best news is that Jesus didn't stay on the cross where he found us. In Jesus' resurrection from the dead, God proclaimed to the world that suffering and death are not the final words. The final word is life. God will never be satisfied with a world that hurts and suffers, and neither can you. Not when there is a risen Savior loose in the world.

It is when we get a glimpse of the risen Jesus that we have hope. He will come to you if you look for him, because he is looking for you. In the words of the apostle Paul, "If God is for us, who is against us? He who did not withhold his own Son, but gave him up for all of us, will he not with him also give us everything else? ... Who is to condemn? It is Christ Jesus, who died, yes, who was raised, who is at the right hand of God, who indeed intercedes for us. Who will separate us from the love of Christ? Will hardship, or distress, or persecution, or famine, or nakedness, or peril, or the sword? ... No, in all these things we are more than conquerors through him who loved us."[7]

Hope comes not from what you know, but from whom you trust. That is what faith provides. It is a way of seeing. But if grace isn't cheap, neither is faith. You may receive it as a gift, but you have to fight to keep it. And the one with whom you eventually have to struggle for your faith is God.

You cannot tell the truth about the harshness of life without realizing God cannot be spared some measure of responsibility. Thus, you will need to forgive even the one who gives your every breath, and you cannot forgive without first blaming. But as you take your case and your wrestling with the question "Why?" into worship, your angry gaze up to heaven is tilted down to the cross. When you see the Son of God hanging there, suffering with you and even for you, your anger turns to thanksgiving, and your fists become the open hands of praise. By then you have realized that it is you who are in need of forgiveness. Not for your anger at God, but for all the dark things the anger made you do before the daylight began to appear—when you saw the Savior's face.

YOUR NEW NAME

At daybreak the blessing finally comes for the exhausted, broken Jacob. It is not the blessing he has spent his life imagining, however. He receives no wealth or esteem, nor any of the success of Esau. No, the blessing is a new name. The Lord said that he would no longer be called Jacob, the Striver. Now he is to be called Israel. According to the text, the name *Israel* means "those who struggle with God." "You shall no longer be called Jacob, but Israel, for you have striven with God and with humans, and have prevailed."[8]

Prevailed? How has this crippled, bankrupt hustler prevailed? He has learned how to cling to God. That was the blessing all along.

It takes a few years and a whole lot of mistakes to learn this. The blessing of life comes not from *what* you are holding, but *whom* you are holding. More to the point, blessings come from the one who is holding onto you.

Sometimes in the Bible, God changes a person's name. Typically this comes at the great turning point in their lives, as it did with Abraham and Sarah, or with Paul and Peter. The new name is given at the point that the individuals are ready to receive the blessing from God. Since this converts everything about them, it is only fitting that they wear a new name. No longer will they pretend to be someone else like the Striver. Now they will be the men and women who cling to God.

Have you ever wondered if God has a new name for you? What would that be? Would it be Grateful or Cherished? Maybe it's Joyful or Merciful. I don't know what your new name is, but I do believe that is what you will be called in heaven because it describes your true, God-given identity. You may live your whole life without knowing that name. You may keep it a secret even if you know what it is, for fear that someone will take it in vain. You may cope with the difficulty of life by pretending that your name is Mean or Frightened or Angry or Hurt. But one of the reasons why Jesus is the Savior is that he insists on calling you by your true name. He knows you. He knows you better than you know yourself. And he calls to you, saying, "You, the Beloved of God, follow me."

After Abram became Abraham, he was never called Abram again. The same thing is true for most of the other people who undergo name changes in the Bible. However, Jacob is only sometimes called Israel in the events that follow this sacred night. At other times he is still called Jacob. It seems he constantly has to choose whether he will accept God's new identity for him. The temptation is always there to pretend he is still the Striver. And Jacob succumbs to this temptation frequently.

Maybe it is because I relate so well to Jacob, but I find his experience with the new name relevant to ours. There is no question but that in Jesus Christ, God has declared that we are new creations. Still, every day brings with it many opportunities to choose if we will act as the women and men that God has created us to be. We can be Joyful in the office full of complaining people. We can be Content in a society that keeps encouraging us to demand more. But it is also possible for us to listen to those around us and to the even more deadly voice that still lurks in our own hearts claiming we are nothing new. These voices tempt us to believe that our struggle is not with God, but with our loved ones, our work, and ourselves. They make us think that we have not yet prevailed and that we must work harder in all of these areas as the Striver before we are going to receive any blessings.

You can go back to pretending that it is all up to you to make a blessing happen. It is a miserable way for someone who has already received the blessing to act, but I do it all the time. I don't get very far with it, however. Usually I only get far enough to realize that I am making big mistakes once again. Most of my big mistakes in life came because I forgot that I am not the Striver anymore. After I remember that God has declared I am now a new creation, it is possible to repent and turn back to my true blessed identity.

The next morning it was time for Jacob to confront Esau. The crippled Jacob hobbled toward him, and when he saw him he fell to the ground bowing seven times as he crawled along. "But Esau ran to meet him, and embraced him, and fell on his neck, and kissed him, and they wept."[9] It is striking that Jacob expected to have a great struggle with Esau, but from him he received grace. He expected to receive grace from God, but that came only through a great struggle. After you have survived the dark night of wrestling with God, it is hard to be afraid of the world around you. That's because you are now clinging to a blessing.

It isn't easy to wrestle with God, and you'll certainly leave the fight with a wound or two. In time, though, you will see that even these wounds are the marks of your blessed salvation.

SETTLING DOWN

Jacob settled in the land where his father had lived
as an alien, the land of Canaan.

GENESIS 37:1

There comes a time when you realize you are not going to get
everything that you wanted. At that point you try to settle for the
life you have.

Your relationships aren't great, but they are comfortable.

The last time you went to the doctor about a nagging ache,
you got a little talk about the aging process.

Your job isn't all you dreamed, but it pays the bills. Well, most
of them.

You no longer wonder if maybe you should go back to graduate school and start over.

So you decide to stop looking for a blessing in the future and
turn your attention back to the life you've already lived. From that
moment you become focused on hanging on to the work, home,
and health that you have, the children you raised, and the world
you know. By the time you come to this point in life, however, you
are already beginning to lose all these things.

Blessings have a short shelf life. They never last as long as we
think they should.

GETTING TO ORDINARY

On first reading, it appears that Jacob's all-night wrestling match with God would make a good ending to his life's story. It is the turning point, and maybe even the climax, but it is not the end of the story. The story continues to describe Jacob's return to an ordinary life.

So much of my ministry as a pastor is about getting people to encounter God in the dramatic moments. Like midwives assisting in birth, I help them through the intense moments of discovering their new life with God. I walk with them through the deep valleys of loss and crisis. I join them on the mountaintops where they give thanks for all they have seen. But most of life is lived in the flat plains, in the place called ordinary.

Getting to ordinary requires leaving behind the dreams of youth. Reality is no respecter of these dreams. They get so hammered over the years they can no longer carry you through the day, much less to a new future.

Sometimes your dreams are interrupted by things you didn't see coming. No one plans on losing their job, or having cancer, or watching their loved ones die early. Sometimes it is God who is the interrupter, and that only adds a spiritual crisis to the loss of the dreams.

But most dreams aren't lost through these gut-wrenching interruptions. Most dreams just fade away.

Eventually you realize the Nobel committee is never going to call. You're never going to become wealthy or stunningly beautiful. You won't ever see your picture on the cover of *Time* magazine. If you're going to make it to the Olympics, you're going to have to buy a ticket to watch someone else achieve glory.

The odd thing is that you don't spend a lot of time thinking about these lost dreams. In fact, you don't even remember the day you stopped think about them. You just lost interest. Now you worry more about keeping the grass green, what you'll do for vacation next year, and when the kids are going to come for

another visit. You hate shopping for bathing suits, gave up on res-
olutions to stay in shape, and would just as soon let the younger
employees work late.

That's when you know your life is ordinary. In the words of
Thoreau, "The youth gets together his materials to build a bridge
to the moon, or perchance a palace or temple on earth, and at
length the middle-aged man concludes to build a wood-shed with
them."

After Jacob's dramatic night of wrestling with God, life sort of
flattens out for him. He reconciles with his brother Esau. He tries
to settle down in a town called Succoth. He pays his bills, feeds
the livestock, and manages the daily life of his family. Nothing is
very extraordinary about Jacob's life from this point on. There are
no more visions, no more angels, no more ladders coming down
from heaven. The challenge he faces from this moment on is what
most of us face most of our lives—just one more day.

This is not to say that life is easy for Jacob now. In fact, his
greatest heartbreaks still lie ahead. There is nothing about ordinary that is easy. As songwriter Bruce Cockburn has written, "The
trouble with normal is it only gets worse." The hard part of life is
not the moments of intense grief, but the long days that are just
vaguely dissatisfying. We know the blessing from God can get us
through the high drama of life. Can it also get us through the daily
places where it feels like the blessing is stuck in a dull routine?

Not even Jesus lived with high drama every day. If we add up
all of the days described in the Gospels, it wouldn't come close to
accounting for the three years of Jesus' ministry. That means he
had a lot of ordinary days when nothing too dramatic was happening. At least, nothing happened that was worth remembering.
I used to wonder a great deal about Jesus' ordinary days. Did he
and the disciples ever have a day when they didn't really do anything more than a little laundry and maybe a late dinner? I have
now come to realize that the Bible speaks as loudly by its silence
as it does in what it proclaims. The silence claims that the ordinary

is just that. It is nothing special, nothing worth noting. Even Jesus had plenty of those days.

It is hard to believe that an ordinary day with Jesus seemed ordinary. If you knew you were going to spend a day with him, you would consider it pretty special. Even if nothing happened that was worth writing down, you would treasure every moment just because you were with him. Well, of course, that is exactly what every follower of Jesus does have this day. But because we consider our lives so ordinary, we don't think there is anything too special about just walking through life with a Savior. That is because ordinary has a way of blinding us to mystery.

DO IT AGAIN

Have you ever swung a small child high above your head, heard the child squeal with fear and delight but then say, "Do it again"? So you do it again, only to hear the same request again. It occurs to you after the fifth or sixth time that this kid is going to last longer on this routine than you are. That's because children are created in the image of a God who takes delight in routine.

You don't have to wake up every morning at five o'clock, fall on your knees, and pray for the sun to rise. The chances are good that if you are able to get up the sun will make it also. G. K. Chesterton has claimed that the sun comes up each morning, not just because of natural laws, but because God says, "Get up there and do it again." All of creation is a testimony that God loves the phrase, "Do it again."

Your life makes that testimony as well. How many years now have you spent your days faithfully going to work, preparing meals, washing the dishes, paying the bills, taking care of the people you love? Nothing extraordinary happened. Nothing life-changing occurred. You just followed the sun through the day, until at last you fell asleep. It was just another day of faithful living. But the next morning a delighted God smiles at you and sends you out the bedroom door saying, "Do it again."

If you ever look closely at the predictable and the routine, you can't take it for granted. Like a small child you will squeal with delight at the blessing that it is. Who is most impressed with the stars of the universe? The astronomers who study them closest and are constantly finding new mystery behind them. Who is most impressed with the intricate workings of the human body? The physicians who are in awe at how all its complex systems work together. Any doctor who is not amazed by the human body is simply not paying attention.

I once had an electrocardiogram test on my heart. After the technician placed a small instrument on my chest, I saw my heart, *my heart*, beating on the monitor. I was overwhelmed. None of us are used to seeing our organs function. But I saw the heart valves that just kept opening and closing, opening and closing, opening and closing. That's their routine. That is also the difference between life and death. I began to wonder how many times those valves had opened and closed in my lifetime. I started rooting for them: "Do it again!"

Most of us don't start out the morning hoping the valves of our heart will keep working. We take it for granted. We assume that the heart will run itself while we concern ourselves with other things. But the routines of the heart are a great blessing. Ask people who've had heart attacks.

How many routine blessings do we take for granted? Some of us take our families for granted. "It's just another routine day with runny noses and arguments and messy houses." But family is a blessing. Ask the people who don't have one. Some of us take our jobs for granted. "It's just another day in the office filled with reports, deadlines, and difficult people." But work is a blessing. Ask the unemployed. And some of us take the church for granted. "It's just another worship service. I'll try to make it next week if I don't have other plans." But the freedom to worship is a blessing. Ask the persecuted church in Sudan or China. We are a people who are blessed beyond our recognition. Nothing that we take for granted has been promised to us.

People who have taken the time to see what they have been given are overwhelmed with gratitude. Since most of life is made up of ordinary days, our best path to joy is to become thankful for the quiet miracles that lie behind the routines which hold life together.

My grandfather had a phrase he used when he was appreciative. He would always tip his hat and say, "Much obliged." People don't say that anymore. My fear is that is because we think we aren't obliged. We think we got it all by ourselves. But we are much obliged; in fact, we are obligated up to our ears to a God who delights in routines and will do it again for us, day after day after day.

This is the grace that lies behind all of Jesus' ordinary days on earth. It was not enough that the Son had to leave his home with the Father in heaven to be born in a lowly manger. When the child became a man, the Father said, "Do it again." So Jesus left his carpenter's home to walk our streets proclaiming God's love and healing. And each day of his ministry the Father told the Son to do it again and again. Until at last he was in a garden begging to be spared the cross. But the Father said, "Do it again." Before Good Friday became a sacred day, it was just an ordinary day, when an ordinary looking man was being crucified on an ordinary Roman cross. Of course, now we can see that nothing about that moment in history was ordinary. It was the extraordinary moment of our salvation.

The same mystery of grace lies behind the days that we judge to be routine and normal. The question is, can we see it? That requires a choice—a choice to see that the greatest blessings in life are not the prizes of hard-fought achievements. Rather they are the gifts of God that come wrapped in ordinary packages. But because we are so busy searching for something more, we have not taken the time to unwrap these blessings. And so we spend most our lives exhausted and spent, looking for the things that are lying at our feet.

WASTING TIME IN THE WILDERNESS

The Bible makes it clear that through all of our ordinary wanderings in life, God has promised to lead us to a blessed future that is filled with hope. The problem with getting to God's future is that you have to pass through a wilderness to get there. It was true with the Hebrews. It has been true in the history of the church. It is true in your life as well.

Most of us want to hustle through the wilderness as quickly as we can. But if we do that, we will miss the blessed reason God brought us there.

There were no back-to-nature movements in biblical days. Ancient people preferred the cities and villages. Nobody wanted to enter the wilderness, because it was a severe land where people easily died. If they had to cross it, they did it as quickly as possible. In the desert they had no reassurances, no security, no reason to think they would be okay. That is why the wilderness is constantly seen in the Bible as a place where faith grows. And faith is our ticket to the Promised Land. All the Patriarchs, Moses, David, Elijah, John the Baptist, Paul, and even Jesus had to spend time in the wilderness to nurture their faith.

Typically when the Bible speaks of wilderness, it is not referring to the lush forests of North America, but to the barren desert of the Middle East. The worst thing about the desert is not the lack of food and water, but the acute loneliness you always feel in your soul. Even if you are surrounded by people, it is hard to take comfort in that when you are in the desert. No one really understands anyone else's grief, because grief is such an intimate feeling. And you always feel grief when you are in the wilderness, because by definition, the wilderness is not the place you want to be. But the greatest source of your loneliness is not that you are alienated from others or even from your own dreams. No, the real reason you are lonely is because you feel alienated from God who left you there.

There may be a few miracles in the wilderness, but the Bible makes it clear that these are easily forgotten in the face of your ordinary daily struggles to keep life going. When you look around your life all you see is a kitchen filled with dirty dishes, or an office filled with boring appointments. You wonder what you are doing there, and you develop serious doubts that you're heading any-where. You miss the place you left behind and pray to return. But God never takes us back to the past.

Our society has trained us to measure our lives by the mark-ers we pass: getting a degree, a job, and a house; and then another degree, a better job, a bigger house. But once your life hits the wilderness, mostly what you do is wander around. It is hard to feel like you are making progress because there are no mile markers in the desert. Each day doesn't seem that much better or worse than the days before it. It certainly doesn't feel like you are mov-ing toward the Promised Land.

The Bible is filled with people who burned up a lot of time before their calling became clear. Only later did it become clear that God had a use even for the dull days. If Moses had not spent forty years in the wilderness trying to keep a bunch of sheep alive for his father-in-law, he never would have known how to keep the Hebrews alive during their forty-year journey through the exact same place. David first had to be a shepherd to sheep before he could become the shepherd-king over Israel. Peter's former life on a fishing boat was transformed into a passion for catching people who were sinking into despair. Paul's many years of study-ing the Jewish law as a Pharisee were constantly redeemed in his debates as an apostle with Jewish Christians. All these people thought they had blown a lot of time before God called them. But something is happening during the long days in the wilder-ness that we cannot see. Something is slowly being created. Our calling.

There is a use even for our mistakes. The awful divorce, the grief, the bad career choices can all be redeemed in time. For now, though, that is nothing more than a faith statement. We can only see the plan of God by looking in the rearview mirror.

I once heard Martin Marty, the eminent professor of the history of Christianity, give a lecture titled *Posterior Dei*. I wasn't quite sure what he was going to do with that title until he got to his biblical text, which was on Moses' request to see God on the desert mountain called Sinai. God told Moses to hide in the cleft of the rocks, and then allowed him to look only after the blinding Shekinah glory had passed him by. When we insist on seeing God we never see more than the *posterior dei*. To demand to know exactly what God is doing along the way in life is to ask to look directly into the face of glory, and that would kill us.

Imagine if Mary knew all that was going to happen to her newly born son. It would have killed any mother to know that. Imagine if the disciples knew about their martyrdom when Jesus first called them off the fishing boats. Would they still have followed? Imagine if as a child you knew every disappointment in life you would face. You would never have left home. Thank God that we only get a little light along the way. According to the psalmist, we get just enough for our footsteps. You are asked only to settle into the day you have today. Tomorrow there will be enough light when you need it.

The only promise we are given is that God will make a way and that he will provide enough water to get us through the desert. When the Hebrews were passing through the long dry years of exile, God cautioned them, "Do not remember the former things, or consider the things of old. I am about to do a new thing; now it springs forth, do you not perceive it? I will make a way in the wilderness and rivers in the desert."[1] The Hebrew is not exactly clear here. Some translations say "rivers in the desert." Others say "streams." The connotation is of a small thread of water, just barely enough to keep us alive. So if the wilderness is an enduring image of the dry place we must pass through, the stream along the way is the persistent thread of God's grace that saves us while we walk along. One dull day after another. This is the stream for which we thirst, like the deer for running water. It gives us hope and waters our dreams for the cherished blessing.

When Jacob left home, he did not go far before he encountered the stream in the desert at Bethel. There, in a dream, God reiterated his promise to bless Jacob. Jacob found the stream again while he was at his uncle's house, when again the Lord stated the promise. After he left Haran and journeyed back home only to confront Esau, his worst fear, the blessed stream appeared yet again when he stayed up all night wrestling with God. By then, he was just starting to realize that the blessing was simply to wander around with God.

The point of being in the desert isn't actually to get to the Promised Land. The point, the blessing, is to become a person with enough faith that you could enter it should it appear. However, once you have discovered that level of faith, you don't really care as much about where you are. By then, you are just enjoying the journey with God.

CHARACTER OVER ACCOMPLISHMENTS

The last words someone speaks to you are always important. You tend to hang on to them as if they were a way of keeping the person near. For that reason when someone is about to speak some last words, they are always measured carefully. Paul's last words to the church at Ephesus provide a summary of the apostle's vision of life. "If only I may finish my course...," Paul concluded, "to testify to the good news of God's grace."[2]

Don't we all want to be remembered for finishing the course that is set before us? I find that after people get to a certain age, they start wondering about what type of legacy they're leaving behind. It's another way of finishing the course. Some want to leave behind grown, healthy children who have children of their own. Others want a building with their name on it. Those who have spent their lives loving Jesus frequently want to leave behind a lasting contribution to his kingdom. That is why they keep asking God what they are called to do along the way in life. "God, I want to make a big difference in this world. And I am willing to pay the cost, like the apostle Paul. Just tell me what you need me to do." We pray like that because we keep thinking spirituality is a matter of what we do, what we save, start, or accomplish. But the longer I work at ministry, the less I am convinced that God needs us to get the work of the kingdom done.

It is hard to be a person of faith, precisely because you are not asked to do great things. What you are asked, is to believe that God can do great things. That is what it means to spend life testifying "to the good news of God's grace."

A pastor once told me that as he walked along the street downtown he began praying that God would use his life for something truly significant. He wanted to build a great ministry. In his prayer he pledged that he would do anything and give up everything to do it. Just then he came upon a large building made up of thousands of small red bricks. He heard the Spirit of the Lord tell him, "I need you to be one of those ordinary bricks." He thought, "No, not that! You need me to be a cornerstone." Of course, that job has already been taken by Jesus Christ. We are called to be just another brick in the wall. It doesn't even matter if some of the bricks in the wall are chipped or even broken. The wall doesn't stand or fall with us. It stands on the Savior, the only cornerstone.

It doesn't depend on you. That statement isn't just our limitation. It is also our freedom, and for that reason, limitations are always a mark of God's grace.

Grace proclaims that what we need is not to accomplish the extraordinary, but to allow the extraordinary to be accomplished within us. Only then will we be of use to what God is going to accomplish in the world. That mission will happen with us or without us. But we cannot receive the blessing of being used by God unless we first present ourselves as the ones who need to receive grace.

It is dangerous to receive grace from Jesus. As the Bible often illustrates, his ways are not our ways. Sometimes the Savior leads us to places we would rather not go, places where our lives get battered and broken. Paul spent his life testifying to the good news of grace to a very ungracious world. For his trouble he was frequently stoned and imprisoned. He faced a struggle almost every day of his life. He was constantly opposed by those within the church and those outside of it. At the end of his life he had no earthly assurances that the fragile church to which he devoted his life was even going to survive. But what does he ask for as an old man? He just wants to talk a little bit more about this wonderful thing called grace. The bruises on his body, and maybe even his soul, were the marks of his salvation. That's the legacy he left behind for the churches he started.

If you grew up in Sunday school, as I did, the phrase "flannel graph" conjures up wonderful memories. When I was in the second grade, Mrs. Williams just loved to tell Bible stories by having the children sit on the floor around a large board with flannel wrapped around it. For each of the characters of the story there was a paper figure that would be placed on the board when we got to their part of the story. With her long bony fingers, Mrs. Williams would rub her hand across the figure until it stayed in place. But she always had trouble with the apostle Paul. He had been used a lot in the stories and he did not smooth out so well. Long ago someone had spilled Kool-Aid on him, which discolored his robe. Two of us once got in a fight over who would hand the apostle to her which resulted in tearing his head off. The tape that then held him together made it even more difficult for Paul to stay in place. But he remains in my mind as the most memorable of all the characters. It was as if his paper-thin life proclaimed a sacred truth to me even then. God is not easy on the people he uses. That is because they are given the most wonderful grace, which they wear on their lives. It is called "character."

There is no easy way to receive character. It is amazing how stained and battered everyone looks in the church. Frankly, the best among us are taped together with prayers and still need a lot of smoothing out. But I wonder if in the eyes of God we are not finally starting to look more interesting. As anyone who has learned faith in front of a flannel graph can tell you, the people who get used the most look the worst. So now we are less impressed with ourselves and much more dependent on the hands of God.

THE GOOD ENOUGH LIFE

The heroes of faith in the Bible were never much use to God until they first developed a grateful heart for all the grace they had received. There is nothing that will mess up our gratitude quite like the resolve to get things just right.

The problem of living in a secular culture today is not that our teachers cannot pray in school, or any of the other "threats" to the faith that Christians tend to worry about. No, the real problem is that we are too easily distracted from what is really important in life. Most of all we are distracted by our resolve to make improvements. The assumption behind all of our technology, progress, and social engineering is that if we just try hard enough, we can also engineer our own lives. This has the effect of constantly preoccupying us with what is wrong.

I think it is high time the church introduces the concept of "good enough." You are not the perfect worker. You are not the perfect mom or dad or child. But you are probably good enough. You do not have the perfect home, the perfect job, or the perfect body. But it is probably good enough. Life only comes with scratches and cracks. That can either preoccupy you with improvement plans, or it can be the opportunity to give thanks to God who insists on loving us only by grace. In time, we may even come to give thanks especially for the flaws in our life, because it is the cracks that allow the light to shine through.

There is so much freedom waiting for anyone who would settle for good enough. It will free you to turn your attention to the perfect work of your Savior.

Not long ago I officiated at a wedding that started as a disaster, but took a nice turn about halfway through. It was a stormy day with the wind and rain pounding against the stained-glass windows. Some of the main city streets had been closed from flooding, which meant the out-of-town guests were hopelessly lost on side streets and would miss the wedding. Also, for some strange reason we couldn't get the candelabra fully lit. So about half of the candles stood in the front of the chapel as burned-out soldiers. By the time we were supposed to start, the flowers had not arrived. Trying to be helpful, our wedding hostess put something together from the previous week's sanctuary flowers, which had a lovely brown tint around the edges. Then the real flowers showed up fifteen minutes after the wedding began. Undaunted, the florist marched down the center aisle to arrange them in front of us. The couple had worked so hard to get this wedding just right. But in spite of all efforts their unforgettable day had become, well, unforgettable.

There are always a few tears at weddings, but this time they weren't from happiness. So I made a few adjustments in the homily and talked about how fitting it was to have an imperfect wedding for what was always going to be an imperfect marriage, just like every marriage. All of the resolve to get unimportant things just right, I said, was about to mess up the important thing, namely, weaving two lives into one flesh. I gave it my best shot, but still I couldn't talk the couple into seeing what was really important. I could still see the anger and hurt in their eyes.

But the moment they turned and faced each other to say their vows, everything changed for them. The groom's eyes watered up with tears of joy as, for the first time, he really saw his beautiful bride. All of his frustration melted away, as he finally beheld the joy of his life. That got her crying, which made me cry as well. They got it, just in time.

Every part of our lives is flawed. So life hasn't turned out the way you thought it would. Those disappointments confront you with a great choice. You can waste every day of your life fixing things. Or you can settle into the life you have been given and give thanks that the flaws just don't matter. It's good enough. But you will never see that until you first turn around and behold the grace of God.

Why would you let what you do not have define you? You have already received the gracious love of God. Do you really need more?

DAILY GRATITUDE

Have you ever noticed that some people have more than their share of problems, but they seem to still be happy, while others with easy lives are not happy? I know a lot of people who got the education and job they wanted, house and car they wanted, even the marriage and children they wanted, but they are still miserable. The thing that distinguishes us in this life is not that some of us are in shambles while others are doing okay. No, the thing that distinguishes us is that some of us are thankful while others are not. Until you become thankful, you will never find joy.

Being thankful is not telling God you appreciate the fact that your life is not in shambles. If that is the basis of your gratitude, you are on slippery ground. Every day of your life you face the possibility that a blessing in your life may be taken away. But blessings are only signs of God's love. The real blessing, of course, is the love itself. Whenever we get too attached to the sign, we lose our grasp on the God who gave it to us. Churches are filled with widows who can explain this to you. We are not ultimately grateful that we are still holding our blessings. We are grateful that we are held by God even when the blessings are slipping through our fingers.

Only when we see this are we able to be truly joyful, because then we have made God our joy. We still cherish the blessings, but not because we have to have them. We cherish them because they are our windows into heaven.

Gratitude is our ability to see the grace of God, morning by morning, no matter what else greets us in the course of the day. That has the effect of making us gracious as well.

Recently I was racing to an important appointment downtown. I was also fighting off a bad cold, and thought I should stop to pick up some cough medicine. The only store that was on the way was a large grocery store. I had just enough time to run in, grab the cough medicine, and still get there on time. But when I got to the express checkout marked "10 items or less: Cash only," I found myself behind a man with twenty-two items in his cart. Not even close to ten.

I began fantasizing about questions I would ask him. "That counting thing sure is hard, isn't it?" Then I saw him pull out his checkbook. I was horrified to find myself reaching up and running my finger across the sign "10 items: Cash only." The checker, who was determined to have a good day, greeted this criminal with a delightful, "Hi. How are you, today? Oh, puppy food. What kind of puppy do you have?" As they began an eternal discussion about collies, I thought I was going to explode. I had to get to an important meeting where I was going to speak about the grace and for-giving love of Jesus Christ!

Finally I got my stupid cough syrup, jumped in the car, and began racing down the road gulping down a few slugs of medicine as I drove. A couple of miles down the road I passed an awful acci-dent. The rescue workers were putting someone in the ambulance as I slowly drove by. It was then that I realized what a fool I had been. I had allowed the clock to get me confused about what is important. I had lost my gratitude for the blessing of another ordi-nary day of life.

Our fast-paced way of life has a way of making the trivial important. We become so angry about things like checkout lines and traffic that when we hear about the true crises of those who are starving to death we have no feeling left in us. We are numb to the pain of the world because we wasted our heart striving to get life just right.

Theologian Karl Barth once claimed that all sin is simply an expression of ingratitude. We have inherited the dysfunction of our parents Adam and Eve in constantly reaching for something more than we have been given. We do that only because we are not truly grateful for a God who has lavished more blessings on us than we can see. Usually, it is not until we have lost the good garden that we start to think of it as paradise.

At the end of the weekend, a man drops off his children at their mother's home. He sits in the car watching the kids skip up the porch steps and then disappear behind her door. He curses himself for being alone.

The mother of the bride sits on the front pew of the chapel. She can't really hear any of the minister's words because they are drowned out by the awful arguments she remembers having with her daughter. She just wanted to help the daughter become a mature woman, but her advice always propelled them into devastating battles. Now it all seems so silly. She just wants another chance to be a good mother. But now her little girl is gone.

An old man sits besides the hospital bed of his dying wife. As the respirator whirls behind him, he pens her a love letter that she will never read. He thinks about all the reports and memos he wrote over the years. He wishes to God that he would have written more love letters while there was still time for her to read them.

It is not until the garden is gone that we realize how good it was.

It doesn't have to be that way. There is an alternative to regret. You can choose today to be grateful, to settle into the blessings that will not last so long. But to do that you will have to find the love of God in what you have. You'll have to settle down.

SETTLING INTO LOVE

We live in a world that keeps telling us we have to prove we are worthy of love. That is why we try so hard to be a success even at the price of losing the blessings we have. That is also why the grace of God is such a mystery to us. How can God just decide to love us? But that is exactly what the cross of Jesus Christ proclaims. It is planted in history as an eternal proclamation that God has chosen to love you. No matter what you do, no matter how far from the garden you roam, this Sacred Lover will find you.

The moment after someone says "I love you" is always thick. It is like the world stops, waiting for a response. And there is only one that will do. When somebody says "I love you" you can't say, "Wait until you see what I accomplish." But that is exactly what we tell God by our compulsive striving. All God wants to hear is, "I love you too."

Growing up, leaving home, finding a job or a friend. Losing your job, your health, or a dream. Living and dying. They are all opportunities to respond to God's love. Every day you are presented with more invitations to say, "In spite of this, because of this, God, I love you."

People who are in love don't think so much about what they want. The thing they enjoy the most is simply the daily expressions of love.

Best of all, when you are in love nothing seems ordinary.

TEN

THE SINS OF THE FATHER

I shall go down to Sheol to my son, mourning.

GENESIS 37:35

Most of life is spent answering questions. "Where will you go to school?" "How will you make a living?" "Who will you marry?" "Can you raise kids and still have a career?" "What about retirement? "What about tomorrow?" The list goes on and on.

We can certainly answer the way we want, but we can't avoid making a response. The questions are etched onto our hearts. Simply by having to respond we illustrate that our lives are not entirely our own. Someone else has set our agenda with these questions. Typically, that someone was a parent.

Since our parents received these questions from their parents, the questions are inherently as flawed as the people who gave them to us. There is no way you can get the right answer, because they are the wrong questions about life. They ask how you are going to earn your blessing.

THE INHERITED STRUGGLE

Having given up on the search for a blessing in his future, Jacob now looks for it in his children. Although this was the time he tried to settle down with his God, these were actually the hardest years in Jacob's life, because now he was destined simply to watch as his children make the same mistakes he had made.

I have seen this drama repeated over and over. By the time most parents have had their great conversion moments with God, it is too late for their children to benefit from it. Some of the greatest saints in our congregation nurture private heartache over the awful choices their adult children are making. They silently watch them spend too much time at work and push their own children to become overachievers. They wonder why they don't go to church anymore. The worst part of watching these mistakes is knowing where they were learned. All the old parents can do now is pray and hurt.

Before Jacob's personal struggles climaxed in his night of wrestling with God, most of his children were already born. The youngest at this time was Joseph, who was six years old when Jacob came to his great turning point in life. That means that the most formative years of these children were spent watching their father trying to hustle the blessing with his work, his collection of wealth, his marriages, and his old struggles with Esau.

That is how children learn the wrong questions about life. Few parents sit their children down and tell them that they should waste their life figuring out how to collect more money, power, or achievements. No, the kids just watch the parents do this. When life is little, it absorbs things like a sponge.

While sitting at the kitchen table doing homework, a young girl watches her father pay the bills. She may look preoccupied with the essay she is writing, but she can't help but hear him complain to her mother, "We simply have to find more money. I can't make ends meet."

A young boy eventually stops running to the door when his mother comes home from work. He has seen her crestfallen, battle-weary face too many times.

As the family drives along in the car the parents begin to speak about a couple who is getting a divorce. The mother says, "I am just so shocked. They seemed so happy." The father responds by saying, "Ah, I knew he was all wrong for her." But in the backseat, little hearts have just learned another bad question—what does it take to make a family break apart?

In our congregation we constantly remind parents that in spite of all the fabulous programs we have for children in the church, the place where faith is really learned is in the home. When we baptize infants in our worship services, I ask the parents, "Will you raise your child in the knowledge of God's grace to the end that they respond with their own faith?" The new parents always affirm their resolve with a hardy, "I will." But occasionally I look over at the old parents who are silently shaking their heads.

The problem isn't the resolve of parents. The problem is their humanity, which keeps slipping out. The knowledge of God's grace gets clouded over by all the other things children learn from Mom and Dad.

Jacob's family provides a textbook illustration of this. After settling in Succoth, his daughter Dinah was raped by a man named Shechem, who was a prince of the region. Shechem's father tried to make peace between the families by proposing a marriage between Shechem and Dinah. The sons of Jacob responded to this proposal "deceitfully" by permitting this marriage only if all the men in the city became circumcised. The men of the city agreed to this condition because they thought it would allow them to eventually absorb all of Jacob's wealth. While all the men were lying around in pain from their surgeries, Simeon and Levi, two of Jacob's sons, strolled through the city, killing them. Then they stole all of the wealth of the city.[1]

It is a sad story of returning evil for evil and trying to outhustle the hustlers. But from where did the sons of Jacob learn these lessons? Are their actions not reminiscent of Jacob's deceitful struggles with his deceitful father-in-law, Laban? Are they not making a familiar response to the same bad question that plagued their father: What must you do to come out ahead in this harsh world?

Another of Jacob's sons, Judah, fathered twin sons who struggled with each other in the womb. Zerah tried to be born first, and stuck just his hand out of the womb. So the midwife tied a crimson cord around it. But suddenly the hand was pulled back in and the other son, Perez, came out first.[2] Of course that set the pattern for the twins' struggle the rest of their lives. Seeing the repetition of his old conflicts with Esau must have broken Jacob's heart.

Later in the story, when Joseph is sold into slavery, he is carried to Egypt by Midianite traders who were Ishmaelites.[3] As Abraham sent Ishmael away from his home, so Ishmael's descendants were now taking Abraham's great-grandson far from his home. You have to believe they took a certain amount of joy in dragging away the beloved son.

This is what the Bible means by claiming that the sins of the father are passed on to the children and to the children's children. We now talk about this as dysfunctional family systems. The children of alcoholics can spend their whole lives reacting to their parents' problems. So can the children of workaholics, sexaholics, and securityaholics. Our parents' story just keeps continuing on and on. That is, unless one of the kids can find a new dream that changes everything.

THE NEED FOR SACRED RITUALS

Jacob was horrified by the actions of his sons at Succoth, but he could not convince them that they were wrong. So he took them back to Bethel, to the place where he first heard the promise that God would simply give a blessing to him and his descendants. There he built a new altar with them, and together they worshiped. Parents cannot undo the bad lessons they taught their children, but they can point them God. Only an encounter with the Sacred will be powerful enough to teach us the right question in life, which is not what must we do, but what can we see? The earlier we establish a pattern of teaching our children to worship, the better the chances are that they will learn how to see the grace that is slowly revealed in their lives.

Worship, if it is done well, is always a ritual. I know that it is quite stylish now to throw out rituals as if they are nothing more than mindless traditions. But they are only mindless if we aren't paying attention. A ritual is a way of rehearsing our identity as a blessed people. It helps us remember who we are. Whether the worship is that of the high church liturgies or the storefront churches of the inner city, all of them are essentially trying to tell the great drama of God's insistence on giving us this blessed thing called grace. The ritual of personal worship allows us to begin every day by hearing God's word of grace before we hear the harsh words of the world around us, and before we form any of our own.

Rituals are not unique to people of faith. We live in a society that has plenty of rituals that will tell us we are someone we are not. Staying late at the office is a ritual. So is complaining when we don't get what we want. And so is trying harder and harder to make the grade. The rituals of the church claim that there is a sacred mystery at work beneath the ordinary routines of life. The rituals of society claim that you are on your own. You can pick which rituals you want to follow, but don't think you aren't following a script that someone else has written.

The key question behind rituals is, who is the author? God or the society around you? Those who insist they are writing their own script in life are just following society's favorite ritual for getting lost. Sometimes people reject sacred rituals because they don't find them "relevant." That's because we live in a society that keeps telling us we can ignore things that aren't relevant to us. But the point of the ritual of worship is not to be relevant to you, but to make you relevant to God.

In the Bible, traditions and rituals are presented not as a conservative effort to hold onto the past. Rather they are a progressive force that allows us to enter new eras of life with history, identity, and a particular interpretation of life. Ritual reminds us that, like Jacob, the story of our lives began long before we were born. It keeps telling us there is a blessing to inherit that has been passed from generation to generation. Only in that blessing will we remember who we are, because we live in a society where that is so easy to forget.

A few years ago the University of California at Berkeley released a study that claims the average person encounters three hundred advertisements in the course of a single day. That is three hundred voices all telling you what to do, what will make you happy, and who you ought to become. Cable television is now providing a hundred channels of programming in many of our homes. The typical grocery store now has at least an entire aisle dedicated to presenting the various options for breakfast cereals. The average paint store will offer you over fifty different shades of the color white.

All of this keeps us busy making choices about things that don't matter. It leaves us terminally distracted from the sacred questions of life.

No one needs ritual more than our children, who are bombarded with interpretations of their lives. The coach has one. So does their peer group, and Nike, and MTV. All of them are different from the sacred interpretation. Unless our youth learn early on who they are by the grace of Jesus Christ, they will be lost in a sea of interchangeable identities.

In Moses' farewell sermon to the Hebrews, he cautioned them to give their children a great ritual of repeating the Sh'ma:

> Hear O Israel: The LORD is our God, the LORD alone. You shall love the LORD your God with all your heart, and with all your soul, and with all your might. Keep these words that I am commanding you today in your heart. Recite them to your children and talk about them when you are at home and when you are away, when you lie down and when you rise. Bind them as a sign on your hand, fix them as an emblem on your forehead, and write them on the door posts of your house and on your gates.[4]

In other words, be sure that your children grow up constantly confronted with the love of God. They had better see it coming and going at home.

Every devout Jewish home repeated the Sh'ma twice a day, at morning and night. Now don't you think that some of their children probably rolled their eyes and said, "Ugh! This is so dumb. Why do we have to do this?" It is not unlike the protests my parents heard when we went through family devotions, or when they made me memorize verses of the Bible, or when they dragged me off to Sunday school.

The chances are good that when our children are free to leave behind our traditions they may do that, for a while. But when life gets hard for them, and it will, they will be able to return to the truth about God's love if they received it through the traditions of early life. They may even return to it with different forms than their parents had, but that is how traditions get shaped. To each generation belongs the responsibility of questioning the adequacy of the received tradition, and to give the gospel story new forms for responding to new questions. But pity those who received nothing that is even worth rebelling against. This is a very dangerous time to be alive without an interpretation to life.

One year during Advent, I was interviewed for a television program about the real meaning of Christmas. The TV station sent a camera crew and a producer along with the interviewer to our church. Before the interview started, I engaged these folks in a casual conversation about Christmas. They were all twenty-something. None of them had a religious background of any sort. One woman thought she may be Jewish, but wasn't sure. Another said to me, "Now, for some reason we make a bigger deal of Christ's birthday than we do Abraham Lincoln's, but I've never understood why."

Our church is across the street from American University. Almost every Sunday I meet another student who strolled into our worship service for the first time. Frequently, I discover it is also the first time they have been in any house of worship. These students are not running away from the church. You have to have a home before you can run away from it. At least the prodigals maintain the memory of the father's home as they wander away. They know it is there when they are ready to return. But how will this next generation find their way home when they realize they are lost? Something has to give us the memory of the Father's love. It is the sacred rituals we provide our children that do that best.

When I was a child, our family, like many, had its little rituals for getting the house ready for Christmas. One of my jobs was to assemble the cardboard nativity scene. It wasn't much. When I saw it again later in life, I was surprised by how small it had become. Every year when I sat on the floor putting tab A into slot A, I thought about preparing the way of the Lord. Oh, I didn't call it that. Most years my big concern was just trying to get the shepherd to stand up straight. But it was as if a holy mystery was being rehearsed in my fragile life even as a child. I was learning how to get ready for the arrival of the Savior. I was learning faith. Later in life, when I had so thoroughly lost my way and really needed to believe that a Savior was coming, that faith was still in my heart, waiting for me to use it.

Of course, parents are not going to be able to give their children rituals of faith unless they believe themselves. That is the tradition that our kids need most. They need to at least believe that we believe. The best way for them to discover that is as they watch our responses to the many challenges and interruptions to life. Do we view these surprises and disappointments as arbitrary disruptions to our plans, or can we see them as more of the unfolding mystery of God's great drama called life? We won't be able to discover that vision unless we have committed ourselves to worship. Since our vision will still be flawed, we had better bring our kids to worship with us so they can eventually see for themselves.

THE CHILD YOU WANT AND THE CHILD YOU HAVE

Nothing created more problems in Jacob's family than his eleventh son, Joseph. There was something very different about this kid. He alone was able to break the cycle of desperation and hustling passed down through the generations. That was because Joseph was a dreamer.

The dreams of Joseph eventually led to the salvation of his family and preserved the blessing for the Hebrew people. But along the way in his life, it seemed like his dreams were responsible for most of his problems. They put him at odds with those who had no dreams. They sounded so outrageous and unrealistic that he was easily dismissed as arrogant and naive. Worst of all, it was because of his dreams that Joseph spent most of his life in exile, far from home.

Jacob loved Joseph more than his other sons, because he was the first son of Jacob's beloved wife, Rachel. That was the primary reason why his brothers, the sons of Leah, hated him so much. Here again, the struggles of one generation were passed to the next.

As the Leah-Rachel tension demonstrated Jacob's struggle between the wife he had and the wife he wanted, so the tension between the brothers and Joseph demonstrated Jacob's struggle between the children he had and the children he wanted. Every child has both Joseph and his brothers wrapped inside. The Joseph part is the part you love the most. Maybe it's because when you see Joseph in your child you are reminded of Rachel. Maybe it's because you are reminded of lost dreams. But for whatever reasons, you make it clear to your child that you love the Joseph part the most.

You affirm that part every chance you get. You talk about the Joseph part to your friends and to his grandparents. You put Joseph's trophies on the mantle. You hang his art on the refrigerator. As Jacob gave Joseph a beautiful coat of many colors, so do you keep trying to dress up the Joseph part of your child. But as your child receives these accolades for Joseph it sets up an internal tension. He is aware that there is more to him than that. He is also Joseph's brothers, the child you do not prefer. He wonders what to do with the brothers. He may try to ignore that part of his life, as you do, but after a while that becomes impossible. The brothers part of him will hate the Joseph part, because you love him more. They will do anything they can to get rid of him. Since there are more brothers than there is Joseph in your child, they will inevitably overpower him in time.

This is one reason why "good kids" sometimes go bad. So many times a desperate couple has come to my office to talk about their problems with a teenager or a young adult. Often they will say, "I don't understand it. He was always such a good, happy child. But it seems like when we sent him to high school a different kid came home. I want the good child back." Earlier and earlier some of our kids are starting to experiment with drugs, alcohol, and sex. Some make mistakes that they will carry with them for the rest of their lives. Their parents are aware of the many ways that the world can wreck a life. That is why they are horrified to watch their kids racing toward the world with outstretched arms. And that is why they want Joseph back. They are terrified of losing him.

When teenagers go through these phases of looking like strangers to their parents, they are essentially trying to work out the internal tension created by the preference for Joseph when they were children. They have now been exposed to enough of the world to find somebody or something that prefers the evil brothers who are tired of being ignored. So the brothers take center stage for a while. This doesn't mean that your good kid has actually gone bad. It just means that Joseph is in exile for a while. If the teenager is fortunate, he or she will eventually come to a point of integration and will recover the part of Joseph that is realistic. But the brothers have to be dealt with first. Since this is hard for a parent (who can't help but prefer Joseph) to do, the kid has to work the struggle out in the privacy of the soul where the tension exists.

Those who spent their formative years with sacred rituals have a great advantage here. In the moments of worship our children are constantly exposed to the only pure form of grace that they will find. Sunday after Sunday they are reminded that God is love. And God has no favorite children. God does not just love the part of us that is good, but also the evil part that no one wants to talk about. Evil is never vanquished by ignoring it, and it certainly isn't going to lie dormant just because we affirm the good within us. Evil is only overcome by love. As much as a parent may want to love even the evil within the young lives of their children, they can't. Not even a parent's love is that powerful. Only the grace of God, discovered in worship, can do that.

Don't worry if the child doesn't seem to pay attention in church. Our congregation, like many, has a children's church program, worship aids for children when they come to "big church," and we do all we can to include them in the family worship hour. But still some parents worry if their kids get the meaning of our rituals. I think that is beside the point for young lives. At this point we just want them to remember the rituals that proclaim God's gracious love. They will come to understand what that means when they need to.

It will be filled with meaning the day they are ready to recover the dreamer in exile. On that day they will need to know how to find a blessing. The rituals will be waiting for them, as signposts that point the way.

DREAMS OF GLORY

We are told that while Joseph was hated by his brothers primarily because their father preferred him, they hated him all the more because of his dreams. In one of these dreams Joseph and his brothers were binding sheaves in the field. Suddenly his sheaf stood up tall, and all the sheaves of his brothers bowed down before his. In another dream it was the sun, moon, and eleven stars that were all bowing before him. The brothers became furious when Joseph told them his dreams. Even Jacob thought they were a bit grandiose.

These dreams certainly appeared to be out of touch with reality. Joseph was just the eleventh son out of twelve boys and apparently several daughters. In his day that didn't mean too much. Everything in his world told him to play by the rules and work hard to fit in as son number eleven. If Joseph would have done this, his life would have been a lot easier. He would have eventually married, had some children of his own, worked on the family farm, and settled into his unremarkable life as one of the boys. That was the plan. Just conform. But nothing will mess up a reasonable plan like a dream.

Dreams are never reasonable. They come to us from God and thus are never something that we would come up with on our own.

Centuries later, another Joseph had made plans to quietly divorce Mary when she told him she was pregnant. It was a reasonable thing to do in his day. By rights, he could have had her stoned. A plan simply to dissolve the relationship is as good a plan as we could expect of him. But in a dream an angel of the Lord told him that this child was conceived by the Holy Spirit and would save the people from their sins. Only with a dream could Mary's husband fulfill his role in God's sacred drama of salvation.

Most of us have far too many plans and not nearly enough dreams. We are never saved by our plans.

We aren't even saved by our plans for achieving the dream. The dreams of Jacob's son were not really that different from the dream he had at Bethel. Joseph was just inheriting it as the next generation. But by this time Jacob had spent his life with plans for achieving the dream on his own, and could no longer recognize the dream for the sacred inspiration that it was. That is because he had seen too many plans.

The most striking thing about God's dreams is that we can only receive them. We can never make them happen, no matter how good the plan is. Joseph had no response when his father and brothers tried to do a reality check on his outlandish dreams. All he could do was tell the dream. This doesn't mean that we don't work for the dream and throw our lives into it. But it does mean that we are constantly aware that none of our work will make the dream come true. We work for the dream, in its service. The dream doesn't work for us.

One of the greatest dreamers of our day was Dr. Martin Luther King Jr. He led a great civil rights movement by always holding his dream in front of the country. Had Dr. King simply devised plans to negotiate seats in the front of the bus for people of color, he would have betrayed the greater dream of a color-blind society. He never reduced his dream to reasonable plans. That is why he was a leader. But even as he walked in the front of marches across the country he was in his own mind always following the Savior who was leading him.

I heard Andrew Young give a speech in which he described an event that occurred early in Dr. King's life.[5] When Dr. King was in Harlem, a deranged man plunged a letter opener into King's chest. They rushed him to the hospital where the knife was removed as carefully as possible. But in order to do that the doctors had to make another incision which cut across the wound. This meant Dr. King was left with a scar on his chest in the shape of a cross. It also meant that every morning when he looked in the mirror to shave, he was reminded that the dream would cost his life. It wasn't about getting what he wanted. The dream was too great for that. It was about the power of the cross to change our world. Only a Savior will accomplish the Savior's dream.

The world has always been hard on dreamers. It was hard on Dr. King. It was hard on Jesus. It was hard on Joseph as well. These dreamers undermine the plans of those who have found a way to cope with the world the way that it is. If you are living in a racist society, you are going to be tempted to resist anyone who would disrupt the inequalities of life that are working in your favor. If you are a Sadducee who has cut a deal with the Roman occupying armies, you are going to be tempted to crucify anyone who looks like a new king. If you are one of Joseph's brothers, you are going to have to get rid of this dreamer who is preferred by the father.

When his brothers saw him coming out into the field one day, they said to each other, "Here comes this dreamer. Come now, let us kill him and throw him into one of the pits; then we shall say that a wild animal has devoured him, and we shall see what will become of his dreams."[6] More plans for more deceit.

As the oldest son, Reuben had the most to lose from Joseph's dreams of glory. If anyone wanted to kill Joseph, you would think that it would be him. But the text makes it clear that Reuben knew this would be too much for their father. So he tried to deceive the deceivers by talking them into just throwing him in the pit without killing him. His plan was to return later and rescue the troublesome dreamer. But while Reuben was away, his brothers sold Joseph into slavery. When Reuben returned to find the pit empty, he grieved deeply for his father.

When we lose the dreamer within us, the heavenly Father will never be consoled by our plans to get him back. It is the planning and scheming that got us into trouble. We can't get out of trouble with a few more plans. Look at David and Bathsheba. Or Jonah. Or Ananias and Sapphira. The only way to plan our way out of sin is with more sin. The alternative would be to simply confess the truth. But after Jacob's sons had lived so long with deceit, after they had learned deceit from their father, telling the truth occurred to none of them. So even Reuben joins in the conspiracy. They shred the special coat, smear it with blood, and tell Jacob that Joseph was killed by wild animals.

As Reuben feared, his father was inconsolable. All his sons and daughters tried to comfort him, but he would not listen to them. He insisted that he would even go to Sheol, to the land of the dead, to be with his son Joseph. It was an interesting thing to say. In fact, Jacob had brought a little Sheol up to his family by teaching them his sins.

WHEN YOUR DREAMS DIE

The story of what happened to Joseph in Egypt is fascinating. But I have always wondered what was happening to Jacob during the long years when he thought his beloved son was dead. It is one thing to hope when you know your dreams are in exile and may one day return. But how do you hope when you think your dream has died?

It is the pastor's great privilege to sit beside people who think they have come to the end of the story. Like Jacob, they assume death has finally won. Someone walks out of a marriage after too much hurt. Someone loses a job. Someone loses hope of ever getting into medical school. Someone who was dearly loved lost a battle to cancer. All of them watched their dreams die. Now the story was over. They thought.

One of the things that has always amazed me about their grief is that there is always some relief in finally getting to the end. As bad as it is to lose the things we cherish, the thing that really drives us crazy is not knowing when the story will end. Happy endings or sad endings we can handle. But stories without endings are impossible.

According to Mark's gospel, Mary Magdalene, Mary the mother of Jesus, and Salome went to the cemetery early one morning to grieve the death of Jesus. Perhaps they had been up half of the night talking and crying like friends and family always do when they come to the end. Maybe they remembered better days back in Galilee when the dream was still alive. How far they seemed from that now. But when they got to Jesus' tomb, they saw that the stone covering it had been rolled back, and Jesus' body was not inside.

A man in a white robe was sitting inside. He said, "You are looking for Jesus of Nazareth, who was crucified. He has been raised; he is not here. . . . But go, tell the disciples and Peter that he is going ahead of you to Galilee; there you will see him, just as he told you."[7] The next sentence is the last sentence of Mark's gospel. "So they went out and fled from the tomb, for terror and amazement had seized them; and they said nothing to anyone, for they were afraid."[8] The End.

That's it? What about the part where Mary met Jesus in the garden and thought he was the gardener, or when Jesus walked beside two of his followers on the road to Emmaus, or when Thomas placed his fingers in Jesus' wounds, or when Peter was forgiven for his denial and affirmed his love for Jesus three times? Mark, finish the story like Matthew does with the great commissioning of the disciples, or like Luke does with the details about Jesus' ascension to heaven. Happy or sad, we can take it either way. Just give us a real ending.

We are not the first to be bothered by Mark's unfinished story. The early church shared our anxiety. Although we do not have any of the original documents of the Bible, even conservative Bible scholars agree that the most reliable and oldest copies of Mark's gospel end at verse eight. But by the second century some of the copies start to include longer endings that add on the parts of the story given by the other gospels. We have never been happy with what Mark has done to us.

Every story has to resolve its ending. Does she survive the cancer or not? Do they stay married or get divorced? Does my teenager return to being a good kid, or do I have to keep living with the brothers of Joseph? We have to know. In fact, we insist on knowing so much that we even prefer to assume that Joseph is dead forever. That is easier than living with uncertainty. I have found that most people prefer the misery they know to the mystery they do not. But Easter will never give us that luxury.

"He has gone on ahead of you to Galilee, there you will see him." By leaving out the details, but giving a promise, what Mark has done is to project the ending of his gospel into your life. A risen Jesus has gone on ahead of you. Since Jesus' story has not ended, neither has yours. That means against all appearances, you have to keep hoping.

On Long Island, where I grew up, there are still some old Victorian homes that were built during the times its beach communities were supported by the whaling industry. Many of these homes have a very small room that sits on the top of the roof called the "widow's watch." It was the place where wives would sit, watch, and pray for their husbands to come home from the sea. Even if they had received word that the ship had been lost at sea, they were expected to keep faith that through some miracle their husband would still return. Those little rooms were built in the belief that there is more than we can see.

Faith means having to watch for an ending that defies all odds. But faith is nothing more than wishful thinking—without Easter.

Down through the centuries, through times of persecution and famine, war and slavery, disease and grief, Christians have never lost hope, because of Easter. Without knowing any of the details of their better tomorrow, they insisted on hoping only because they believed a risen Savior was waiting up ahead for them. That is why some couples still try even when marriage is hard. That is why cancer patients fight their way through chemotherapy and radiation. It is the only thing that explains the resolve of parents who will go to Sheol to find their lost sons and daughters. It even explains the faith of those who bury loved ones, believing they will see them again someday.

Mark could not give us the end of the story. That is because he wanted to give us this thing we need even more, called hope. But hope has an inseparable companion: mystery.

BREAKING THE PATTERN OF SIN

I want to believe that even though Jacob had no concept of Easter, he did have the faith to keep hoping in his God. He had seen some pretty incredible signs of God's intent to bless him against all odds. After wrestling with God all night, no one could possibly be the same again. Through these lifelong struggles to believe that he would receive a blessing, Jacob had to know by now that God's mercy was stronger even than the sins that the old hustler father had passed onto his children.

There has to be something that can break the pattern of sin from generation to generation. There is. That is exactly what the mercy of God can do. The question is, do we have faith in it? Or better yet, does faith have us?

We speak of faith as if it were a possession. We encourage each other to "have faith," or sometimes to "keep faith." The last thing you want to ever do is "lose your faith." This reduces faith to another tool we may use to achieve our goals in life. The Bible, however, doesn't describe faith as if it were something we owned. It claims that it is something that owns us.

Actually faith is similar to another virtue called love. We don't say that someone has love for someone else; rather we say that one is in love. The difference is more than semantics. By claiming to be in love we admit that we are overwhelmed by a great commitment to another person. Sometimes it hits us at first sight, and at other times it develops more slowly, but at no time would we claim to be in perfect control of the love. More honestly, we admit that the love has the power to control us. Similarly faith in God is a wonderful commitment. It may come slowly or in a moment, but once it has hold of us it changes everything. Like being in love, we don't know where the faith will lead us, what it will cost, or how it will all end. That is what creates the drama of people who live by faith. We may even struggle with our faith, or try to deny that it exists, but the Bible claims that it is pretty hard to fall out of faith.

The Bible also distinguishes between the faith of individuals and The Faith of the people. Your personal faith is always shaped and molded, and sometimes carried, by The Faith of the covenant people. In biblical times people were not as preoccupied as we are about individuals. They understood the individual only as a part of a much bigger whole. This left them secure in the knowledge that their ability to believe did not depend on what was going on within their own souls. When you have too much fear and confusion to keep believing, you have to lean on The Faith that is rehearsed through all the people's rituals.

Jacob struggled with his faith in God's blessing his whole life. With the apparent death of Joseph he reached the greatest challenge he would ever face to keep believing. But he couldn't stop believing even if he wanted to. The Faith of Abraham and Isaac had hold of him.

If we read ahead to the end of the story we discover that when the brothers told Jacob that Joseph was alive in Egypt, "the spirit of their father Jacob revived."[9] Then he wanted to go immediately to Egypt to see his lost son. It was a better ending than he had thought.

You can spend a long time with your spirit still in Sheol while you wait for the story to end. But what ultimately matters in your struggle to keep believing is not your own faith, but the faithfulness of God.

ELEVEN

FAITH IN GOD'S FAITHFULNESS

I wait for your salvation, O LORD.

GENESIS 49:18

The story of Jacob's life isn't really about Jacob. It's about God's determination to give us a blessing. Jacob tried so hard to pry that blessing out of God's hand. But for all his efforts, all Jacob really accomplished was to hurt himself and the people around him.

There is another way.

THE HUSTLER AND THE DREAMER

The life of Joseph is a critical chapter in the story of the blessing. He demonstrates that no matter how dark the day there is still the possibility of living with hope—but only if you are really clear that the blessing will come simply because God is faithful in giving it to you.

There are some interesting parallels between Jacob and Joseph's lives. Both received a great dream of being blessed early in life, and that dream changed the course of their journeys till the day they died. Neither deserved the dream as a birthright or by any other rights. Both endured great difficulties with brothers and the many others who did not live with a dream from God. Both spent the majority of their lives far from the home they dreamed of inheriting. The most important parallel is that the dream wasn't really about either one of them. It began before they were born, and it continued in the hearts of those who followed them. They just got to hold it for a while.

But it is the differences between the father who spent his life hustling God and the son who spent his life responding to God that are most striking. By putting them beside each other, we are confronted by the life-defining choices we must make as well.

Achieving Vs. Receiving

Jacob was all initiative. By contrast, in the entire story of Joseph's life, not a single act of initiative is recorded. But at the end of their lives, Jacob died hungry in exile while Joseph died inheriting every blessing Jacob so desperately craved. This is not because Joseph just stumbled into them, as Esau appeared to do. Joseph endured a much harder life than his father. But he went through it all with open hands. That is why God could remove the heartaches and replace them with blessings.

In Egypt, Joseph experienced great injustices. After working hard to succeed in Potiphar's house, he was falsely accused of seducing Potiphar's wife and was thrown in prison.[1] Although he was a dutiful prisoner and a good friend to the other inmates, he was still forgotten and left in prison.[2] Even though he had risen to a position of great prominence in Pharaoh's court, he was still shunned by the other Egyptians who considered it "an abomination" to eat with him.[3] When a famine arose in the Promised Land, Joseph's brothers came to Egypt to find food. They didn't recognize that the man with whom they were negotiating was the brother they had sold as a slave.

Through all these sorrows, Joseph continued to believe in the dream of receiving God's blessing. He never limited the blessing to the injustices of the day. That is why he could live a much harder life than his father had, but without any of the bitterness and anxiety that plagued Jacob. Waiting on God, Joseph simply watched the great drama of his own life unfold.

Joseph was not a striver, but he became the second most powerful man in the known world. He was not a schemer, but through the providence of God, he rose to just the right position in life. He was never the aggressor, but he humbled the brothers who hurt him by the powerful act of forgiveness. Joseph got to the place in life Jacob could never achieve. And he got there simply by making good responses to the initiatives of God.

Faith is demonstrated not in what we accomplish, but in how we respond to the unpredictable drama of life. It doesn't matter how hard we knock ourselves out trying to make a blessing happen, it simply can't be done. Blessings only come by the unfathomable mystery of God. They are a grace in that they save our lives. The best measure of how far you are roaming from that grace is how hard you are working to stay in control. In my own life I have realized that I work hardest to make sure things are running just right when I have not spent enough time hanging around the Savior. One of these days I am going to find the faith to respond to a difficult dilemma by saying, "I can't wait to see how Jesus bails us out of this one."

After Pharaoh met Joseph, he asked his servants, "Can we find anyone else like this—one in whom is the spirit of God?"[4] Joseph didn't impress Pharaoh by his achievements. Pharaoh had seen plenty of that. So have you. So have the people you are trying to impress. People with full résumés are a dime a dozen. But it is rare to find someone with God's Spirit. You can't achieve that. You can only receive it, and once you have, you will become quite distinctive in a society of overachievers.

Deceit Vs. Honor

If you take on the burden of making your dreams come true, you'll eventually find it necessary to bend the truth. You'll flatter the people you work for, explain away your failures by shifting blame, and make promises you can never fulfill. Since we live in a world of half-truths and sort-of truths, you won't find it difficult to excuse yourself. But a half-truth is still a total sin. It is wrong not only because you are not telling the truth, but more importantly because you are not counting on God to save the dream. Once you compromise the truth, you are compromising the dream. At that point it becomes something less than the dream you received from God.

Jacob deceived his father and his brother, his employer and his wives. Through it all he was deceiving himself with the fantasy that the blessing could be hustled. In spite of all his striving, we have no record in the Bible that Jacob enjoyed his life. He spent so much energy on spinning stories that there was no room left in his heart for joy.

I have found that deceit is like holding a beach ball under water. With a good deal of effort and a lot of concentration, you can do it for a while. But truth is buoyant. It always rises to the surface in time. Those who believe in the buoyancy of the truth are distracted neither by holding their own lies under the water nor by trying to wrestle the truth free from others. Rather than wasting time trying to convince people what they didn't do, they are free to do the right things, confident that the truth will eventually come to the surface for all to see.

Joseph was able to live an honorable life because he could live by the truth, even when that came at great cost. He simply continued to do the right thing and left the implications to his God. There were times when that landed him in slavery and jail. In time, the truth eventually lifted him to a position of great honor in Pharaoh's court. But Joseph was a man of honor long before he was given the honorable job.

I sometimes meet with ministerial candidates who have gone to seminary primarily because they want to live an honorable life. There is nothing, nothing about being a pastor that will make you honorable. It doesn't come from the job. It comes from letting the grace of God transform your own life every day, as you confess the dishonorable things you do. Pastors who haven't had their own souls straightened out before they climb into a pulpit will find they are creating an amazing amount of damage in their churches.

In his final temptation, the devil took Jesus to the top of a high mountain and offered to give him all the kingdoms of the world if only Jesus would worship him. Jesus rebuked the devil by saying he could serve only God. It is significant that he didn't say he wasn't interested in the kingdoms of the world. That's because he couldn't. Christ came to the world to save the world and would have loved to have all its kingdoms without having to go to a cross. That's why the devil's offer was tempting. The most deadly temptation is not about our goals, but about the means we will use to get to them.

Those who have committed themselves to great dreams will not likely be tempted by an offer to start running numbers for the mob. But they will be tempted to think they have to be realistic about what it's going to take to make their great dreams come true—a few compromises, hard work, and just a little sacrifice of honor. It is all a way of making a bad deal with the devil.

This is why so many good people become mean. They want to do something wonderful but become so obsessed with their goals that they hurt others and themselves in the reckless pursuit of them. We see this in the church all the time. The wild-eyed elders demand the budget they want even if it means cutting other programs. They may get it, but along the way they have corrupted the church into something less than the body of Christ. Parents make the same mistake when they yell at their kids to be nice. Friends lose honor when they spill secrets under the guise of prayer requests. Colleagues at work lose honor when they view each other as assets or liabilities. The great tragedy is that when we sacrifice our honor to get what we want, we end up with neither our honor nor the blessing we wanted so badly. The devil has deceived us. He doesn't own the world and certainly cannot give it to us.

Having the Blessing Vs. Being the Blessing

When the blessing first came to Abraham, God made it clear that he and his descendants were being blessed, "so that you will be a blessing ... and in you all the families of the earth shall be blessed."[5] The blessing was never meant to be a prized position of the children of Abraham. It was supposed to give them a mission to be God's blessing to all the families of the earth. Jacob never understood this. Joseph never forgot it. One spent his whole life trying to wrestle the blessing away from the families of the earth as he struggled to get to the right place in life. The other spent his life being God's blessing to all he met, even when they were responsible for keeping him in the wrong place.

Few people think they are in the right place. When I try to get to know someone, often they tell me where they are from. "I moved here five years ago from Ohio." It's part of their story, and it's the part that claims they aren't at home. Others may be living in the right place, but they aren't working in the right place. Or their relationships haven't grown to the right place. Or maybe they haven't even arrived at the right place with God. We all know something about exile.

In the sixth century before Christ, the Hebrew people were dragged from the Promised Land by the Babylonians. They longed for the day they could return home. During this time the prophet Jeremiah spoke some of the most encouraging words in the Bible. "For surely I know the plans I have for you, says the LORD, plans for your welfare and not for harm, to give you a future with hope."[6] This verse has continued to be a great inspiration to people of faith. We have a copy of it hanging on one of the walls in our home. I love the hope and reassurance that it provides. But I must admit that I keep forgetting about the rest of the words Jeremiah continued to speak. Since the future belongs to God, the prophet reasoned, those who are held captive in a place they do not want to be should settle into the life they have. According to Jeremiah, God wanted them to "build houses and live in them; plant gardens. . . . Take wives and have sons and daughters." Then comes the real surprise. "Seek the welfare of the city where I have sent you into exile, and pray to the LORD on its behalf."[7]

If we really believe that the future is filled with hope, we are free from worry about where today is heading. Knowing that God alone controls tomorrow, we can be a blessing in the day that we have. We can even bless the people who have hurt us, because we are not anxious about contributing to their victory. They don't win. But they will never become convinced of that unless you bless them.

I met a pastor of the Chaldean Church in Baghdad shortly after the Persian Gulf crisis. I asked him about the conditions of life for the church in Iraq during the war. He responded by saying that it was very difficult for them because the Muslims considered them Western sympathizers.

"How did you survive?" I asked.

"We did what the church has always done when it is persecuted. We fed the hungry, gave shelter to the homeless, and developed orphanages. It was such a powerful testimony that eventually even the government brought people to us."

Never settle for hanging on until things improve. No matter how bad it is, there are still opportunities to live and serve today. If you miss them, you miss the point of your life.

Distractions Vs. the One Thing

Since Jacob wasn't very good at receiving, he could never find a blessing in the things he had been given. This preoccupied him with searching for the blessing in others things—leaving home and trying to return home, moving around, changing his job, getting married, and then getting married again. His days were spent on a trail of restlessness.

While waiting by the baggage claim carousel at the airport, I saw a suitcase that was coming apart at the seams. Too many things had been crammed inside and the case couldn't hold it all. The owner had tried to secure it with duct tape, but not even the tape could keep everything inside. So we all watched someone's clothes slowly spill out while the broken suitcase glided along the carousel. There, I thought, goes contemporary life with way too many things crammed inside. We've tried every way we can to keep it all taped together, but some days it feels like it is coming apart at the seams.

The amazing thing about this is that we still live with guilt over the things we have not accomplished. There is always one more phone call to make, one more appointment to keep, one more project to complete, one more goal to achieve. So in spite of the fact that we are already dropping some valuable things, we do the crazy thing of cramming still more in our stressed lives.

There is another way to live. It isn't complicated, but it is hard. You just have to travel more lightly. But to do that you have to be clear about what you will need for the journey.

If you study the lives of the great saints in history, you'll notice that the older they got the more focused their lives became. They are less distracted by the agendas of others for them. They are even less distracted by the many unrelated interests of their youth. In maturity, they all became centered on one idea or vision. They possessed it. Or more to the point, the idea possessed them, and everything in their lives had to be related to this one great idea, or they let it go. For St. Augustine, the great idea was the confession that the heart is restless until it rests in God. For Luther it was the doctrine of justification by faith. For Martin Luther King Jr. it was the great dream of a color-blind society. For Mother Teresa it was giving dignity to the dying.

History has made these people great, but at the time they were making decisions about how to use their lives they weren't thinking about greatness. They were just choosing to commit themselves to a dream. It doesn't matter how old you are, there are still plenty of days left to make a great contribution to your part of our world. But you have to find the one idea that overtakes your life and let go of the rest.

How do you find that one thing? You don't. It finds you. So many times people will come to see me wanting to know God's will for their lives. They show me their many charts. They let me read their journals. They pull out their pro/con lists and their personality inventories. But still they are not sure. That is because they are not yet possessed by a great idea.

Well, how does that happen? How did it happen for the great leaders of the historic church or for the apostle Paul? How did it happen for the young mother who sacrifices a career and dedicates her life to the idea of raising healthy children? How did it happen for the retired businesswoman who committed her second half of life to a whole new mission? None of them went shopping for great ideas. All of them devoted themselves to knowing God. In doing so, they found God's dream. Along the way they found the dream in the thing that was before them. Then they knew what to do.

Joseph went through several different job descriptions in his life, but through all of them he was focused on the great idea of being a faithful servant. He served his master, his jailor, Pharaoh, and then his hungry family. Through all of these jobs, he was serving his God. The great idea that possesses you is your true vocation. It is the dream that focuses your life. It can't be contained by a job, which is never more than a temporary means of fulfilling your dream.

GIVING UP HOPE OF A BETTER PAST

Joseph is almost too good. His responses to overwhelming hardship are so spiritual that you may wonder about his humanity. Actually, he was plagued by one struggle that stayed with him through most of his life. He couldn't let go of his past. His father was always so focused on the future that he could never enjoy the gift of the day. But it is clear that Joseph's days were pierced by memories of his father's home. As a result, he always remained an exile from the place he wanted to be.

There is nothing that will make you an exile from the present quite like leaving your heart in the past. Some are held captive by past glory. They carry in their hearts the great achievements of the past like tattered old résumés that have no room for new adventures. More of us, though, are held captive by the hurt of those we once trusted. Those sins are hard to forgive. Almost as hard as our own sins.

I have found that just because we hear forgiveness is possible, it isn't easy to believe. If you are struggling with your own sin, it is hard to believe you can be forgiven, because you think you don't deserve it. You don't. You don't understand grace if you are not completely humbled by it. If you are struggling with the sin of someone who hurt you, it may be hard to believe you can offer forgiveness. That only means you are not ready to forgive. Some rush to forgiving too quickly. You can't forgive unless you have first told all the truth about your hurt.

Some of us say we have forgiven, but actually we have just chosen not to do the hard work of forgiving. Instead we make a little record of the offense. This can take up a lot of time.

When I was a young boy, my mother collected S&H Green Stamps. These stamps were given by grocery stores as a bonus for making purchases. Once a sufficient number had been collected into books, you could cash them in for gifts at an S&H Redemption Center. My job was to help my mother by licking the stamps and placing them into books. That is how some people forgive. When a small offense occurs you say, "Forget it." But in your heart you lick a stamp and put it in your little book. Another offense occurs, and another stamp goes in the book. Eventually the book gets full. Then one day when the person who has been making these small transgressions is late for an appointment, you are horrified to watch yourself overreact with a screaming tantrum. What happened? You just cashed in your book. Forgiving and forgetting may not be the same thing, but those who have truly forgiven aren't interested in keeping records of sin.

Most of the transgressions that are hard to forgive are not little. They are huge, and the hurt runs pretty deep. There is a time for expressing your anger. However, you are never going to be able to forgive until you are tired of being angry. How long do you really want to live with rage at your ex-spouse, the supervisor who fired you, or the parent who was too hurt to love you? It just compounds the injustice and allows them to keep hurting you.

GOD INTENDED IT FOR GOOD

The people who are successful at truly forgiving have found a sacred perspective to the sins and offenses that they are struggling with. They have discovered their own forgiveness when the Son of God went to the cross to stretch his arms out to them. In embracing that gracious love, they are changed. So much of the love fills their heart that it starts flowing over into their other relationships. Equally important, they have discovered that God has a use for everything, even the deep hurts created by the careless sins of others.

After enduring a life of hardship and then finding himself in a wonderful new life in Pharaoh's court, Joseph had two sons. He named the first son Manasseh, which means "making to forget." When the son was born, Joseph said, "God has made me forget all my hardship and all my father's house." The second son he named Ephraim, which means "to be fruitful." Then Joseph said, "God has made me fruitful in the land of my misfortunes."[8] Eventually, Joseph got to a place in his life when he could see the ways God was redeeming the hurt in his life.

The most profound illustration of this is found in his conversation with his brothers near the end of the story. The brothers are terrified of what Joseph will do to them in retaliation for all the hurt they caused him. But Joseph responded by saying, "Do not be afraid! Am I in the place of God? Even though you intended to do harm to me, God intended it for good, in order to preserve a numerous people, as he is doing today."[9] Through most of life we can't see the good intentions of God for the evil that sent us far from where we wanted to be. That is why we must forgive along the way, leaving it to God to work all things, even evil things, together for good.

Stephanie is a forty-year-old woman in our church who came to see me because she was tired of being angry at her divorced parents. Their reckless pursuit of passion tore apart their home when she was a teenager. Her father moved out, remarried, and relocated across the country. After the divorce there was never enough money, enough guidance, and most importantly, enough love. Stephanie was only eighteen when she entered into a disastrous marriage that fell apart five years later. She now believes that she was looking not for a husband but for her father. The bad marriage was only one of a litany of mistakes that she blamed on her parents. When I asked her how God may be using her past pain for good, she got a confused look on her face and our appointment ended abruptly. A month later she came to see me. She said she tried to make a list of the ways God had redeemed her parents' divorce. Frankly, it wasn't a very long list, but the first item caught my eye. "I found the heavenly Father who will never abandon me." Stephanie still has over half her life to enjoy. She can only do that if she sees how incredible a blessing she has received in finally knowing who her real father is.

WHY DOES GOD USE EVIL?

I keep wondering why God chooses to use the evil of others to get us to the right place in life. Maybe it was necessary for Joseph to rise to a position of influence in Egypt to save his family from starvation. But why did he have to go through slavery and jail to get there? Why do good people have to be pushed around by mean people? Surely there is an easier way for God to get us to the places we are supposed to be in life.

The story of Joseph illustrates that this is another one of my bad questions. Or at least it isn't the right question. It certainly isn't the question God is asking, who is much more concerned with who we are than with where we get to in life. The good intention of God is not finally to get us to the right place, but it is to mold us into a people who live only by our faith in the faithfulness of God. Wherever that happens is precisely the right place for us to be.

When John Calvin first went to Geneva to lead the reformation there, he failed terribly. In 1538 he was thrown out of the city by those who resisted his message, and he had to live in exile in Strasbourg. To pay his bills he sold his precious theology books and tutored students. It was a dark time in his life. It was also the time in which he learned the most about the sovereignty and faithfulness of God. When he was able to return to Geneva three years later, he arrived as a different man. The first time Calvin was in Geneva he wrote his first edition of *The Institutes of the Christian Religion*. Frankly, it is not an impressive treatise. It was not until after his experience in exile that he was able to write the theologically rich edition that has continued to teach millions of Christians how to know a sovereign God.

Dietrich Bonhoeffer's life offers an even more dramatic illustration of how God uses evil. He was a German pastor who participated in the resistance movement against Adolf Hitler. Shortly after Bonhoeffer became engaged to the love of his life, Maria von Wedemeyer, he was arrested and sent to prison. On December 19, 1944, he wrote one of his last letters to her before he was executed. In this love letter, he included the following poem, which he also wrote in jail:

> Although the old year still our hearts oppresses,
> and still of evil times we bear the weight,
> O Lord bestow upon us that salvation
> for which our troubled souls thou didst create ...
> The candles brought by thee into our darkness,
> let them today burn clear and warm and bright.

And bring us, if thou wilt, once more together.
Thy light, we know it well, shines in the night . . .
By kindly powers so wondrously protected,
we wait with confidence befall what may.
We are with God at night and in the morning,
and just as certainly, on each new day.[10]

It would be possible to view the love between Bonhoeffer and his fiancée as a tragic story that was cut short by Hitler's gallows. Or we could view their resolve to love as a testimony to a faith that grew strong when they were in the hands of an evil man. Their faith has outlived Hitler, as it did Herod and Pilate, and every tyrant who has ever intended evil.

Once you have come to believe that God is with you, the only wrong place to be is away from that blessing. What can evil do to pull you away from a Savior? Nothing. In the words of Paul, who at the time was in the hands of Nero, "Who will separate us from the love of Christ?"[11]

GREAT IS THY FAITHFULNESS

During the long years while Joseph was in jail, he had plenty of time to develop faith in God's resolve to bless him with a better future. He had fallen about as far as any human can fall. He had experienced one injustice after another. He was never sentimental about this and longed to be free once again. But he never despaired. That was because he chose to believe in the faithfulness of God.

In *Addiction and Grace*, psychiatrist Gerald May has claimed that no matter how oppressed we may be, we always maintain the capacity to envision another way of life. This is what Gandhi was referring to when he used the term "soul force" to describe his "internal undying ember of freedom." It is also what Martin Luther King Jr. meant when he said, "I refuse to accept the idea that the is-ness of our present nature makes us morally incapable

of reaching up for the ought-ness that forever confronts us."[12]
These great, heroic visions in a better tomorrow could only have
been made by people who, like Joseph, had spent time in the bottom places of life.

Unless you make a choice to believe in God's resolve to give
you the better tomorrow, you will never be able to trust it when it
arrives. The volatility of life will create too much doubt, and you
will never be able to embrace the blessing when it comes because
you will be too afraid of losing it again. Joseph believed in God
when he was in jail. That was the only way he could really believe
in God when he had risen to power. We sometimes say that it is
easy to trust God when everything is going well, but that has not
been my experience as I watch people. Unless we have already
found God's faithfulness when everything is going badly, we will
live with great anxiety when things are going well. It is hard to
enjoy a blessing if you are worried about losing it.

Marriage provides a good illustration of this.

Paul and Beverly were a middle-aged couple who loved each
other deeply. They had not been members of our church for long
when Bev was diagnosed with Lou Gehrig's disease. It broke all
of our hearts to watch the disease slowly shut down her body. Her
sharp mind still worked fine, but it was trapped inside a body that
wouldn't allow her to communicate. Through the long months of
the worst part of the disease, Paul's devotion to his beloved wife
only grew stronger. Every time someone from the church stopped
by their house, he could be found at Bev's side telling her he loved
her even after she could no longer say, "I love you, too."

After Beverly died, it was hard for Paul to be in church. It
wasn't that he doubted God as much as he found he missed his
wife most at church. Worshiping God had been such a central part
of their lives together. Paul continued to come to church because
he knew he should and because he frankly didn't know where else
to go. As the confused disciples once said to Jesus, "To whom can
we go? You have the words of eternal life."[13] Sometimes that is

nothing more than a faith statement. This was one of those times for Paul. I would see him sitting on the back pew, always crying quietly through the worship services. Jean and Ted were another couple who were in love with each other. The highlight of Jean's life had been when she sat in the front pew of the church one beautiful Saturday morning to watch her daughter get married. Less than a year later Ted was suddenly killed in a horrible plane crash along with her daughter and new husband. Then Jean sat in the front pew again, this time staring at three caskets.

In the year that followed the pastors and caregivers of the church did all we could to guide both Paul and Jean through their long days of grief. They were surrounded by the loving community of our church, but grief is still such a lonely feeling. Neither of them had ever felt so very much alone.

Then one Sunday after church, I noticed that Paul and Jean were spending a long time together at the coffeepot in the fellowship hall. I mentioned this to one of the other pastors, who said he had seen them talking a long time in the parking lot the previous week. We tried the best we could to stay out of this wonderful new relationship, but it wasn't easy. Soon their tears in church gave way to holding hands through the worship services. Eventually I received the phone call I had been longing for. "Pastor, we were wondering if you would perform our wedding."

I was so excited when the day finally came to marry Paul and Jean. But I wasn't prepared for what would happen during the ceremony. I got about halfway through the service before a question developed in the back of my mind: "How can these two find the courage to go through this again?" I tried to push it out of my thoughts and continue leading the ceremony, but it became unavoidable the moment they faced each other to say their vows. Paul started to cry when he got to the part "... in sickness and in health. ..." I could feel the tears welling up in my own eyes. Then Jean cried her way through saying, " ... till death do us part." At that point I could no longer speak. I looked out at the congregation who were all crying so hard they could no longer listen. So we just stopped the service and cried for a while.

Now the question was demanding a response. If any couple knows what marriage càn cost it is these two. Clearly they are aware that one of them will have to go through all of the grief again someday. How could they find the courage to risk loving again? The answer to my question came when Paul and Jean then faced the congregation as we sang the hymn they had selected— *Great Is Thy Faithfulness*. It was because they had found the faithfulness of God in the darkest days of their grief that they were now able to receive a new blessing. They know they will have to give it back someday. But they also know God will be there when that day comes.

There is always a great risk in receiving a new blessing. The risk isn't *if* you will have to give it back, but *when*. It doesn't matter when that time comes, it will always seem too soon. For that reason, many people choose to live without the blessings and simply hold onto their loneliness, their hurt, and their anger. But those who find the faithfulness of God at the bottom of life are more likely to take risks with the rest of life. That is not because they think things will necessarily improve for them, but it is because they now know they can never lose the most important blessing, which is the love of God.

TWO DIFFERENT ENDINGS

When Jacob died in Egypt, he used his final breath to give his sons instructions on how he was to be buried. He wanted them to carry his body back to the Promised Land so he could be laid to rest next to Abraham and Sarah, Isaac and Rebekah, and Leah. It was the conclusion we would expect to a life of struggle and striving. In the end he died far from the place where he wanted to be. So he demanded to at least be buried in the right place. This is the way all strivers think. You have to do the best you can while you have life, because you are going to be dead for a long time.

When the last day comes and life is over, all that is left is to give final instructions on where to put the body.

When Joseph died he left behind a different legacy. He gathered his brothers together and told them, "I am about to die; but God will surely come to you, and bring you up out of this land to the land that he swore to Abraham, to Isaac, and to Jacob."[14] In the end, what Joseph wanted his family most to know is that this was not the end to their great drama with God. The dream that began before they arrived would outlive him. In the meantime, he would die as he had lived, trusting in God's faithfulness. He then told the Israelites, "When God comes to you, you shall carry up my bones from here."[15] It is significant that Joseph would not allow his family to bury him in the Promised Land until God had come for them. Even in death, Joseph was still waiting on the initiatives of God.

THE BLESSED ENDING OF LIFE

The end of the story does not come with your death. If you have decided to live out the biblical story of life, you will have to turn to the book of Revelation to find out how the story ends. There we find the vision of John, which was recorded to give hope to a church that was being severely persecuted. At that time so many Christians were losing their lives for the faith, but as John's vision made clear, death was not the end.

Your story began with the creation of God. It had its most decisive chapter with that God coming for you in Jesus Christ. According to Revelation, the story then ends with you joining a great multitude crying out,

> Salvation belongs to our God
> who is seated on the throne,
> and to the Lamb!

In response, the angels around the throne of God fall on their faces and begin singing a hymn of thanksgiving.

Amen! Blessing and glory and wisdom
and thanksgiving and honor
and power and might
be to our God forever and ever! Amen.[16]

Notice that in the end, no one is impressed with how hard
they worked or struggled to get a blessing. No, in the end the only
thing that everybody in heaven is doing is giving thanks for the
salvation they have received. According to John, even this end is
only the beginning of enjoying God forever.

If you choose to believe that the story ends with your salvation, you can give up the hustle today. It's the only way to receive
the mystery of today, even the mystery of your death, with expec-
tant faith. It is all an opportunity to enjoy God, who alone will
carry you to the blessed end.

NOTES

Chapter One—Born to Strive

1. Genesis 25:23.
2. 1 Corinthians 15:19.
3. Psalm 1:1.
4. Matthew 5:3, 5.
5. Genesis 12:2.
6. Matthew 3:17.
7. Ephesians 2:8.
8. Isaiah 40:31.

Chapter Two—Learning to Pretend

1. Genesis 25:27.
2. Genesis 25:29–34.
3. Genesis 12:1–3.
4. Genesis 27:11–13.

Chapter Three—Leaving Home

1. Genesis 27:41.
2. John 20:17.
3. Matthew 4:18–22.

Chapter Four—Rehearsing the Dream

1. *Washington Post*, March 28, 1997, p.1.
2. 1 Corinthians 15:14.
3. Genesis 28:13–15.
4. Genesis 28:16–17.
5. Psalm 27:4.
6. Genesis 28:22.
7. Genesis 28:20–21.

Chapter Five—Struggling with Love

1. Genesis 29:1–30.
2. 1 John 4:8.
3. 1 Samuel 18:1.
4. Genesis 29:17.

Chapter Six—Struggling with Work

1. James W. Michaels, "Oh, Our Aching Angst," *Forbes*, 150:6 (September 14, 1992), p. 47.
2. Luke 12:13–21.
3. John 21:18.
4. Exodus 3:4–5.
5. Exodus 3:7–10.
6. Viktor E. Frankl, *Man's Search for Meaning* (New York: Simon & Schuster, 1963), p. 104.
7. 2 Timothy 4:7.
8. 1 Peter 2:9.

Chapter Seven—Struggling with Ourselves

1. Romans 7:15.
2. Matthew 4:6.
3. Lewis Smedes, *The Art of Forgiving: When You Need to Forgive and Don't Know How* (Nashville: Moorings, 1996), p. 178.
4. Genesis 32:12.
5. Genesis 32:24.
6. 1 John 4:18.
7. 2 Corinthians 4:7.
8. 2 Corinthians 4:8–9.
9. Matthew 26:23.
10. Matthew 27:4.
11. Frederick Buechner, *Wishful Thinking: A Theological ABC* (New York: Harper & Row, 1973), p. 15.

Chapter Eight—Struggling with God

1. Genesis 22:26.
2. John Updike, *Rabbit Run* (New York: Fawcett Columbine, 1960), p. 237.
3. Job 6:4; 7:11.
4. Job 13:4–5.
5. Job 42:5.

6. John 1:1, 14.
7. Romans 8:31–37.
8. Genesis 32:28.
9. Genesis 33:4.

Chapter Nine—Settling Down

1. Isaiah 43:18–19.
2. Acts 20:24.

Chapter Ten—The Sins of the Father

1. Genesis 34:13.
2. Genesis 38:27–30.
3. Genesis 39:1.
4. Deuteronomy 6:4–9.
5. *Congressional Record*, September 13, 1995, p. E1777.
6. Genesis 37:19–20.
7. Mark 16:6–7.
8. Mark 16:8.
9. Genesis 45:27.

Chapter Eleven—Faith in God's Faithfulness

1. Genesis 39.
2. Genesis 40.
3. Genesis 43:32.
4. Genesis 41:38.
5. Genesis 12:2–3.
6. Jeremiah 29:11.
7. Jeremiah 29:5–7.
8. Genesis 41:50–52.
9. Genesis 50:19–20.
10. Dietrich Bonhoeffer and Maria von Wedemeyer, *Love Letters From Cell 92*, edited by Ruth-Alice von Bismark and Ulrich Kabitz (Nashville: Abingdon, 1992), p. 270.
11. Romans 8:35.
12. Gerald G. May, *Addiction and Grace: Love and Spirituality in the Healing of Addictions* (New York: HarperCollins, 1988), p. 18.
13. John 6:68.
14. Genesis 50:24.
15. Genesis 50:25.
16. Revelation 7:10–12.

SACRED THIRST

Meeting God in the Desert of Our Longings

M. Craig Barnes

Jesus once said, "Those who drink of the water that I will give them will never be thirsty." So why are Christians still thirsty? We throw ourselves into church work, Bible studies, prayer, missions, fellowship. Yet still we search restlessly for something more. What are we missing? Perhaps the answer is, more of Jesus. Church meetings and programs, ministry, Christian counseling, and home groups are all good, but they are not him.

In *Sacred Thirst*, author and pastor Craig Barnes brings us face-to-face with our desperate longing for God. Like the woman at the well, we have tried to satisfy our parched souls with so many other things. But when we get to the bottom of our desire, we find Jesus quietly waiting with his living water, and he offers us intimate communion with the Father, Son, and Holy Spirit.

If you know there must be more to the Christian life than what you are now experiencing, and if you long to encounter God instead of only acquiring more knowledge about him, *Sacred Thirst* will point you toward the living God. Draw deeply from God's grace and accept what only he can offer—living water that will truly satisfy.

Pick up a copy today at your local bookstore!

Hardcover 0-310-21955-8

We want to hear from you. Please send your comments about this book to us in care of the address below. Thank you.

ZondervanPublishingHouse
Grand Rapids, Michigan 49530
http://www.zondervan.com